The Inclusive Pulpit Journal
Resources for Community Church Worship

The Inclusive Pulpit Journal
Resources for Community Church Worship

Published by
Community Church Press
P.O. Box 486
Longmont, CO. 80504
Phone: (815) 464-5690
Fax: (815) 464-5692
Email: icccnow@sbcglobal.net
Web: www.icccnow.org

ISBN:

Printed and bound in the United States of America

The Inclusive Pulpit Journal

Resources for Community Church Worship

Volume 25, SUMMER 2021

Edited by
R. Tim Meadows, Ph.D.
Senior Pastor
Protestant Community Church/Cathedral of the Woods
Medford Lakes, NJ.

Pamela Jones
Business Administrator
Protestant Community Church/Cathedral of the Woods
Medford Lakes, NJ.

Cindy Conolly
Administrative Assistant/Wedding Administrator
Protestant Community Church/Cathedral of the Woods
Medford Lakes, NJ.

International Council of Community Churches

FROM THE EDITORS

You hold in your hands the final edition of The Inclusive Pulpit Journal. This final edition is special and looks a bit different than previous editions. This edition begins with a dedication to Bob Puckett who joined his beloved Jane in the larger life with God in 2020. Bob was a longtime editor of the journal and a faithful participant and advocate of the ICCC. We also celebrate Charles Trentham's legacy by republishing a sermon and pastoral prayer given by his wife Ann to the ICCC on the occasion of his untimely death. This edition features all of the award winning sermons through 2020 that were selected as recipients of the Charles Trentham Homiletics Award. This award was established by the Trentham family to remember Charles and to honor those who work diligently at the art of preaching. The final section of the journal contains entries of sermons and meditative pieces for the year 2021. We commend to you the reading and engagement of the content of this journal edition. May the grace and peace of God fill you as you read and reflect.

The International Council of Community Churches

With offices located in Frankfort, Illinois, The International Council of Community Churches is a network of interdenominational, community churches located throughout the United States and in seventeen countries around the world devoted to the prayer of Christ, "that they all may be one." Its primary purpose is to be a grassroots demonstration that the ecumenical spirit works.

The International Council of Community Churches is affiliated with the World Council of Churches, the National Council of Churches, and Churches Uniting in Christ.

Our Mission
As people devoted to following Christ we are committed
- *To community*
- *To treasuring diversity*
- *To living our faith in service and love.*

Our Vision
- *To affirm individual freedom of conscience*
- *To protect and promote congregational self-determination*
- *To proclaim that the love of God, which unites, can overcome any division*
- *To be an integral partner in the worldwide ecumenical movement.*

Contact ICCC at 21116 Washington Parkway, Frankfort, Illinois 60423-3112. Phone: (815) 464-5690, Fax: (815) 464-5692, Email: icccnow@sbcglobal.net. Information about the Community Church Press and other publications may be found at our website, http://www.icccnow.org/.

Contents

Charles A. Trentham Homeletics Award Winners 1997-2020

Contents continued

DEDICATION

This final edition
of
The Inclusive Pulpit Journal
is lovingly dedicated

to our

eminent editor emeritus

Rev. Dr. Robert M. "Bob" Puckett

1926 - 2020

A man who filled our heads with wisdom, our
hearts with mirth, and our world with joy!

Rest In Peace

Bob!

Acknowledgements

We are grateful to the pastors, preachers, and friends of ICCC churches who have graciously provided manuscripts suitable for publication in this volume of *Inclusive Pulpit*.

The members of ICCC Community Church Press Editorial Board read the sermons submitted for the Inclusive Pulpit and determine the winner of the Dr. Charles A. Trentham Homiletics Award each year. We are grateful to the members of the Board who have served with the editors in selecting the sermon which best reflects the spirit and values of the Community Church movement. The Charles A. Trentham Award is announced each year at the annual conference banquet. Award guidelines and a list of previous recipients can be found on the final pages of this volume.

A Word From Our Executive Director

Greetings,

As I write this message, we continue living through a time of pandemic, a time where we are living in some continuing isolation and social distancing. It has also been a time of innovation as pastors and congregations have learned to embrace social media for their worship services, bible studies and other congregational activities. I have taken the opportunity to watch several worship services and to experience a variety of preaching and worship styles. It has been wonderful "to hear" different preachers and their preaching styles.

I hope you will take the opportunity "to hear" the preachers who submitted their sermons for this issue of The Inclusive Pulpit. May your spirits be renewed and refreshed by God's Word being preached through these pages.

I want to thank the pastors and members who contributed to this issue, and the Rev. Dr. R. Tim Meadows and the staff of Protestant Community Church/Cathedral of the Woods in Medford Lakes, NJ. for their service again in editing this issue of The Inclusive Pulpit.

Phil Tom
Executive Director

REMEMBERING
DR. CHARLES A. TRENTHAM

The following sermon and pastoral prayer was shared as a gift to the ICCC shortly after Charles Trentham's death by his wife Ann. Both the sermon and the prayer capture the fervent pastoral heart that Charles possessed as well as his keen intellect and love for those in need. Read either as an introduction to Charles by one who did not know him, or as a reminder to those who were among his friends, both pieces reveal an excellent preacher and pastor with true character.

The Editors

The Meaning of the Ascension
MARK 16:19, LUKE 24:50-51, ACTS 1:9-11

Delivered by Dr. Charles A. Trentham
July 12, 1992 at the Church of the Redeemer, Knoxville, TN

A new resident moved from a small town to a large city. He was so intimidated by the tangled traffic that he called the Chief of Police to ask when he could most safely move his van across the city. The Chief replied very decisively, "Seven o'clock on Sunday morning. The Catholics will be at Mass, the Protestants will still be asleep, and the Jews will be on the golf course."

The chief thought he had covered all the ecumenical bases, but when the newcomer pulled out on the main street at seven o'clock on Sunday morning, he was broadsided by a Seventh-Day Adventist going to work.

If you asked what this story has to do with my sermon, I will have to confess that it is nothing more than a labored facetiousness in my attempt to gain your attention. Now to the more substantial.

In the age when church historians were formidably intelligent and scrupulously honest brokers of the truth about church origins, there was a man named Harnack who after meticulous research concluded that there is no evidence that what we call the Apostles' Creed was ever recited in the first seven hundred years of the life of the church of the living God.

Nevertheless, there was what might be called a baptismal quiz which contained some of the items of the Apostles' Creed to which candidates for baptism into the church must subscribe. Moreover, for at least thirteen hundred years since the days of Charlemagne there have been congregations of Christians just as there are multiplied millions today who include in their worship this confession of faith: "I believe in God, the Father Almighty, and in Jesus Christ, His only Son." The creed then continues to cite certain

13

things about the Son, including: "He ascended into heaven and is set down at the right hand of God."

In 1967, a Bishop in the Anglican Church, John A. T. Robinson, who had written the book *Honest to God*, joined with his American disciple, Jim Pike of the Grace Cathedral of San Francisco, to declare that thinking of Jesus ascending into heaven was no longer appropriate in this age of space - that thinking of God as "being up there" is a limiting concept of a localized God. They chose to replace this part of the Apostles' Creed with the God who is down here - the God whom Paul Tillich called "ground of our being".

They might have reinforced their argument by using the original version of our Lord's Prayer. In this initial record, Jesus did not speak in the language of the Bible, but in Aramaic and the literal translation of His salutation, "Our Father who is throughout the universe."

My first response to the Bishop's position was that being down here is just as much a spatial concept as is being "up there" and therefore just as limiting. The more I think of Jesus, the more reluctant I am to give up my upward look and my belief that Jesus ascended into heaven. At the same time I reserve the right to say what I mean by that and to tie it in with that sublime statement of Jesus: "And no man hath ascended into heaven but He that came down from heaven even the Son of Man who is in heaven" (John 3:13).

The Meaning

May I then tell you what the Ascension means to me?

Look first at Luke's brief account. This physician/historian gives it to us in five brief verses - two in his gospel (Luke 24:50-51) and three in the book of Acts (1:9-11). He tells us that forty days after Jesus rose from the dead, when He had finished talking with His disciples on the Mount of Olives, a cloud lifted Him out of their sight and carried Him up into heaven. An angel then told them that Jesus would come back the same way he departed.

Some say that the recorded accounts are not exactly alike. Would you not expect that? Caught in the midst of such maddening events as these writers were, what surprises me is that there is any order at all in their stories. Look at what they had witnessed - the brutal crucifixion of their best friend and of the best man that ever lived. Then they had seen Him raised up from the dead. Should this not have driven them out of their depths and made their writing incoherent?

The story of the Ascension is not a scientific account of a man who defied the law of gravity. It is a statement of faith in a man who had said. "And I, if I be lifted up from the earth, will draw all men unto me" (John 12:32).

14

Neither the discrepancies in the details nor the scientific objectives need dim the devotion of the person of faith who holds on to the picture of Jesus ascending into heaven and sitting at the right hand of God. This picture has been tenaciously guarded by the Christian community and presented in the stained glass windows of churches and cathedrals around the world.

Why?

The answer is that the picture of Jesus ascending into heaven says something about Jesus that Christians believe and which cannot be said in any other way.

What the Ascension Says

Look then at some of the things this picture says.

I. It says that God has a way of lifting up that which the world puts down.

The world has always put down the best there is. It has a way of crucifying the things of God. Crucifixion was the world's way of putting down the best that God had to offer. But from God's point of view, it was God's way of lifting up before our eyes an undreamed kind of love - a love which withheld not God's own beloved Son but freely delivered Him up for us all. Why people reject the very best remains a mystery. But that they do so remains a fact.

We see this in the realm of music. The music of Johann Sebastian Bach was rejected. For one hundred years it was buried in a grave until Mendelssohn raised it from the dead. Then it ascended on high and now all music is judged by Bach's work.

So Jesus, once rejected, despised and spat upon, crowned with thorns, nailed to a cross, put down into a tomb of oblivion, now reigns in heaven.

Where is Heaven?

Heaven is where God is. Where is God? God is everywhere. When we affirm our belief in the Ascension, we are saying then that we believe that Jesus is supreme and that He reigns not only where we are located but that He reigns everywhere, even where He has never been heard of.

Take, for example, the law of gravity. It reigns everywhere - not only in scientific centers where people understand it, but here, where few of us really understand it, and in the jungles, where nobody understands it. Still it reigns and everyone must come to terms with it.

15

So it is that Christians believe that God's reconciling love in Christ reigns everywhere as the stirring, solid, unshakable reality with which we must deal.

He reigns in sick rooms where there seems to be nothing but pain and sorrow and agony until we cry out in prayer. He reigns in mental hospitals where there seems to be nothing but derangement, where the whole human enterprise seems to be denied any significance at all because it is so twisted. He reigns even in houses of prostitution and crime where goodness is almost unheard of.

How?

Do you ask how can this be? Like the sun, Jesus can be shut out of life, but also like the sun, He continues to sustain even those who shut Him out.

If you believe this, something begins to happen in your life in this very moment. You may see no signs of the presence of Christ. But the Ascension says whether you see it or not, He is there just the same. Your willpower may shut Him out the way you would pull down the blinds and shut out the sun, but He continues to sustain even those who shut Him out.

Jesus reigns but not in overbearing splendor. He reigns in the simplicity in which He lived. He reigns in humility and love. Should He come to us now, He would wear no crown or colorful vestments. He would wear the overalls of a carpenter or the simple robe of a teacher.

When we say that we believe that Jesus ascended into heaven, we are saying that the qualities that were in Him - His humility and love - are the things that make the world to round.

One of my favorite popular songs is "Love Makes the World Go Round". It is the love that was in Christ which holds our world together and our hearts in hope.

We cannot prove that Jesus reigns anymore that a musician can prove that Bach's music reigns. All he can say is, "listen to the music." And all we can say is, "Look at Jesus." Enter into His life. Let His way be your way, and then decide whether or not He reigns.

II. The second thing the Ascension means is that God needs us.

Immediately before He ascended, Jesus said, "You shall be witnesses unto the uttermost part of the earth."

A few years ago, a stormy debate occurred over what was called the "Death of God Theology". Tom Altizer and William Hamilton were trying to Americanize what Dietrich Bonhoeffer meant when the Man for others died

16

- that God was calling Man to come of age and stop expecting God to do what God has called Man to do.

Jesus as God incarnate of earth soothes our sorrow, heals our wounds and drives away our fears. Nothing can ever change that. But when Jesus was lifted up into heaven, He no longer had human hands with which to hold our hands when we are in trouble. He asks for our hands to do that for Him.

III. The final meaning of the Ascension of Jesus is that we now have a champion - a forerunner who has gone before us - whose forborne voice assures us that we can never outdistance God. It means that we can never be alone, neither on earth nor in outer space.

We who believe in the Ascension of Jesus, then, mean by this conviction that He who once was rejected now reigns - that we are never alone and that God needs us. If we are ever to really meet Him, we must meet God not only on earth where we need Him, but also in heaven, in that realm where He turns His work over to us, where "His servants shall serve Him and they (and they alone) shall see His face" (Revelation 22:3-4).

When we believe in the Ascension of Jesus, we are lifted up with Him into heavenly places of service. As Robin Clack said, "The longer I serve Him, the sweeter He grows."

On earth Jesus came among us as a man who ministered to our needs. And still when we are in need we turn to Him instinctively. When we are sick, we turn to Him for healing. When we are guilty, we turn to Him for forgiveness. When we are discouraged, we ask Him to lift us up. In His incarnation He stooped to our needs. He called us out of our preoccupation with our needs to meet His needs. He called us out of our preoccupation with our needs to think of His needs that we may be drawn into a redeeming devotion to Him.

Here, for example, is one who is addicted to drugs. To divert her narcotic obsession, she takes up painting. She does this for her own sake so that she might break her pernicious habit. But she discovers that she cannot break the habit until something higher happens. She begins to be mesmerized by the beauty of her painting. Then painting takes her up. The beauty of her painting becomes so important that is transcends her addiction to drugs. She becomes obsessed with painting for its own sake.

All of us are inclined to take up God because we believe He can help us over the hurdles of life. Then we find one day that God takes us up into a higher realm where He asks not so much what He can do for us but what we can do for Him. Isn't that the best kind of redemption?

17

Pastoral Prayer

Charles Trentham
July 12, 1992

We come, O Lord, before your throne of grace on behalf of others.

We think of those in special trouble and distress of body, mind or heart.

We think of those who have been disappointed in love and are more lonely now than they have ever been before. Help them to call up that special courage which you alone can give and in which they can live productively until the one you made for them shall appear.

Bless the homes in which someone has died and in which those who are left are trembling in bewilderment.

Bless the homes where someone must sit by the bed of a loved one to wait for the end to come.

Bless those who are ill and whose pain intensifies with the passing of the hours.

Grant to those of us who must travel your journeying mercies until we are together again.

Through Jesus Christ our Lord. Amen.

CHARLES TRENTHAM HOMELETICS AWARD WINNERS 1997-2020

1997

The Never Ending Journey
PSALM 72:1-14, MATTHEW 2:1-12

Rev. Virginia Leopold 1997
Protestant Community Church
Medford Lakes, New Jersey

Every year on the closest Sunday to Epiphany, each member of our congregation receives a paper star with a word, such as "courage," or "hope," or "clarity," on it. The word becomes that person's spiritual focus for the year, whether it represents a trait they already possess, or an area with room for growth, or something to be given to or received from others. In some cases, it is readily apparent to the star holder what their word signifies. Others take all year to clarify its meaning and purpose. This tradition has had a powerful influence on many of us over the years.

Twelve days after Christmas is the traditional time when the Christian Church celebrates Epiphany, which means "Manifestation," since the light of Jesus Christ manifested itself in the darkness. But it has also been called the Feast of the Three Kings, since this is also when we celebrate the arrival of the wise men.

From childhood on, all of us have had firmly implanted in our minds the Christmas scene. We've seen it in movies and pictures, on Christmas cards, and in countless pageants. There is the lowly stall with Mary and Joseph watching over a sleeping Jesus in a manger. They are surrounded by cows and donkeys and sheep. A star shines in the sky, there are angels somewhere in the vicinity, and several humble shepherds complete with sheep come to gaze and adore. And, of course, three kings bearing gifts!

Unthinkable that they shouldn't all be crowded into that typical Christmas tableau, but the picture isn't accurate. We've compressed the story, accordion-pleated all into one glorious evening of busy confusion. But the wise men did not miraculously amble into the stable on the evening of Jesus' birth. Their arrival has been conjectured as being anywhere between 40 days to one year after the Holy Night.

There were vast distances to travel over unknown terrain. Their destination was unsure. They were at the mercy of the elements and the countries through which they traveled. This much we know – they came from afar. Their name "wise men" is a translation of the Greek word Magi, a name by which they are often known and from which have come the terms magic and magician. They were probably members of an Oriental priestly caste who were familiar with astronomy or astrology, and had been taught by dispersed Jews to expect the coming of a Savior, a universal King. Some sign in the heavens convinced them that such an event had taken place.

How long did it take them to prepare for the journey? How long to set out? To cross the great distances from different directions? A very long time probably passed before the weary travelers arrived in Jerusalem. Tradition has it that there were three kings (one old, one young, and one black) from Egypt, Indian and Greece, with the names of Melchior, Caspar, and Balthazzar. But there is no basis of fact for any of that. In truth, we do not even know that there were three wise men. The Bible gives no number. There could have been two, or a whole caravan. We get the number three because just three explicit gifts (gold, frankincense, and myrrh) are mentioned.

We do not know how long they remained in Jerusalem once they arrived there. What we do know, according to Matthew's Gospel, is that when they followed the star to Bethlehem, they found Mary with Jesus in a house. Yes, in a house – not a stable or barn. Perhaps the Holy Family had stayed in Bethlehem for Mary to regain her strength, or perhaps they had returned to Nazareth after the birth, but had journeyed back to Bethlehem a year later for the Passover.

Regardless of the question of these facts, all Christians who hear this story instinctively recognize its value, importance and meaning: the triumph of goodness over evil; the call of God upon diverse lives, bringing them from far away and by many ways to worship the Christ; and the sense of awe and wonder, thanksgiving and worship that surrounds the birth of this child.

And I'm thinking too that our false perception of the Magi's miraculous appearance on the eve of Christ's birth completely negates the arduousness and peril, the cost of sacrifice of the wise men's journey. This was no quickie trip to the mall. To outfit a caravan cost a fortune. There were provisions to secure. Family and friends were left behind, traded for a distant journey across the wilderness on the strength of a sign! There was no star to follow. They didn't see a star again until they journeyed to Bethlehem from Jerusalem. They followed their heart's call over the desert.

I'm reminded of a wonderful story of a missionary woman who taught in a mission school. One of her favorite students was a young boy. At Christmas time he presented her with a beautiful, perfectly shaped seashell. She knew there was only one beach where he could have obtained this shell, but that was over 30 miles away and the boy had no means of traveling that far. When she asked him about it, he admitted that he had walked the 30 miles there and the 30 miles back in order to obtain the shell. She was aghast. "But that's so far," she said. "Why ever did you do it?" He answered gently, "Long walk part of gift."

So, too, I think, for the Magi all the long distance and all that long time for one purpose – *worship*. Not to serve Him, not to seek favor from Him or to rule in power with Him, but to worship and adore.

I am struck by the startling comparison the wise men's journey has with our own spiritual journey. So many people never realize the cost and commitment the Magi undertook. They mistake the Christian walk as being easy and quickly attained, without incident, or snag, without dry deserts to cross, without nights so black you can't see where you're going. There seems to be this misconception that all one has to do is say you're a Christian, or come to church occasionally on Sunday and – ALLAKAZAAM! – one can change the course of mighty rivers, bend steel with bare hands and leap tall buildings with a single bound, landing squarely, smartly, neatly, at the side of the manger, bathed in the glory of the presence of God.

But while those people are trying to take the leaping shortcuts, down below are those awestruck Magi, plodding the long trail, living out their lives on that journey. Faith and devotion is not that starburst in the sky. Faith is the vision, the eyes to see the star even when it has faded from the sky. Yet, still it burns in one's heart and leads you on.

And just as the long walk was part of the boy's gift to his missionary teacher, so too is our life's journey the gift we give to Jesus. There is a purpose in the journey itself. God gives the sign, and we may stay or we may journey. We will face hardships, both natural and humanly–created, for the journey leads to life for all who venture it. And there will be some who, like Herod, react with hatred and hostility, who would gladly destroy this Jesus Christ who interferes with their lives. And some, like the chief priests and scribes, will react with indifference. They will pass on by Jesus, for He means nothing to them.

But there are the wise ones who will react with adoring worship, who desire out of love to lay at Jesus' feet the grandest and noblest and best gift they can bring. And I am convinced that the best and grandest gift is the gift of ourselves, our whole selves, our life's journey. Not a life lived selfishly for our own pleasure, which at the end we plop down as a paltry gift for the Christ Child. Rather each twisting and turning of our way, each valley and mountain, each joy and sorrow, each act of charity and love, care and outreach, of our whole voyage through life is the only gift that is worthy to place before this Jesus. Anything less comes from a heart that doesn't fully understand what God has done for us through the birth of His Son.

There are the famous to whom we can point and say, "See? They understood. They gave or are giving their lives as gifts." Mother Theresa, Martin Luther King, Florence Nightingale, John Wesley, Billy Graham. But most are not famous. Most are quiet, dedicated people who have given their lives in service as the greatest gift they could give.

Today each of you has received a special Epiphany gift. Perhaps the word on your star is not one you would have picked for yourself. Maybe you don't understand the meaning or relevance of the word at all. But in the days to come, as you meditate on it and think of ways in which it might apply to you, as you wonder on the mystery of how God intends to make use of that gift in your life, perhaps you will find your star gift helping to develop a focus of your relationship with God that lasts throughout the year. In responding to the star word, simply receive it as a pure gift. Your response to it, however, becomes in turn your gift to the Christ Child this year.

Each year at Epiphany, I am reminded again of one of my favorite stories. Written over 100 years ago by Henry Van Dyke, it is too long to read in its original version, but because it is so relevant to today's lesson, I will share a condensation. The story is called *The Other Wise Man:*

In ancient Persia there lived a certain man named Artaban. He was a tall, dark man with brilliant eyes. His robe was pure white wool thrown over a tunic of white silk, and a pointed cap rested on his flowing black hair. It was the dress of the ancient priesthood of the Magi.

One December night he told his friends, "My three friends are watching at the ancient temple in Babylon. If the promised star appears, they will wait ten days for me, and then we will set out together for Jerusalem to worship the One who shall be born King of Israel. I have sold my possessions and bought these three jewels – a sapphire, a ruby and a pearl – to carry them as a tribute to the King."

While he was speaking, he thrust his hand into the inmost fold of his girdle and drew out three great gems – one blue as a fragment of the night sky, one redder than a ray of sunrise, and one as pure as the peak of a snow mountain at twilight.

As Artaban watched the eastern sky that night, a steel-blue spark was born out of the darkness. It pulsated in the enormous vault. "It is the sign," he said. "The King is coming, and I will go to meet Him." And so he rode hard and fast.

At nightfall on the tenth day, Artaban was only three hours away from the temple where he was to meet his friends. Suddenly, his horse stood stock – still before a dark object in the road. The dim starlight revealed the form of a man lying there moaning.

Artaban's heart leaped to his throat. How could he stay here to care for a dying stranger? What claim had this unknown fragment of human life upon his compassion or his service? The three wise men would go on without him. Should he risk the great reward of his faith for the sake of a single deed of charity?

"God of truth and purity," he prayed, "direct me in the holy path, the way of wisdom which Thou only knowest." Then he dismounted and carried the man to a little mound at the foot of a palm tree. Hour after hour he labored to comfort and help the stranger. At last the man's strength returned.

To Artaban he whispered, "I have nothing to give thee in return – only this: I am a Jew, and our prophets have said that the Messiah for whom you seek will not be born in Jerusalem, but in Bethlehem. May the Lord bring thee in safety to that place, because thou hast had pity upon the sick."

It was now past midnight. Racing to the meeting place he found the three wise men had gone on without Artaban across the desert. Artaban covered his head in despair. "I must sell my sapphire and buy a train of camels and provisions for the journey."

He arrived in Bethlehem three days after the three wise men had departed from the Christ Child. He entered the open door of a cottage and found a young mother singing her baby to sleep. In her gently speech, she told Artaban, "Joseph of Nazareth took the Child Jesus and His mother Mary and fled secretly in the night."

Suddenly there came the noise of wild confusion in the streets of the village, and a cry: "The soldiers! The soldiers of Herod! They are killing our children!" The young mother's face grew white with terror, and she clasped her child to her bosom and crouched in the darkest corner of the room.

Artaban went quickly and stood in the doorway. The soldiers came hurrying down the street with bloody hands and dripping swords. As the captain of the guard approached Artaban said in a low voice, "I am all alone in this place, and I am waiting to give this jewel to the prudent captain who will leave me in peace." The captain stretched out his hand and took the ruby. "March on!" he cried to his men. "There is no child here."

Artaban turned to the East and prayed, "God of truth, forgive me. Two of my gifts are gone. Shall I ever be worthy to see the face of the King?" Weeping for joy, the woman said, "Because thou hast saved the life of my little one, may the Lord bless and keep thee; the

Lord make His face to shine upon thee and be gracious unto thee; the Lord lift up His countenance upon thee and give thee peace."

Artaban, the other wise man, traveled from country to country, searching for the King. In all this world of anguish, though he found none to worship, he found many to help. He fed the hungry and clothed the naked and healed the sick and comforted the captive. Three and thirty years passed. Worn and weary and ready to die, but still looking for the King, he came for the last time to Jerusalem. Excitement was flashing through the city's crowd.

"Have you not heard what has happened?" they asked Artaban. "Today they are crucifying Jesus of Nazareth, who says He is the Son of God and the King of the Jews." Artaban's heart beat unsteadily. "I have come in time to offer my pearl in ransom for the King's life," he thought.

A group of soldiers came down the street dragging a girl. She broke suddenly from her tormentors and threw herself at Artaban's feet. "Save me," she cried. "I am to be sold as a slave. Save me!" Was this his opportunity or his last temptation? Twice, the gift he had for God had gone to serve man. He took the pearl from his bosom. Never had it seemed so luminous, so radiant. He laid it in the hand of the girl. "This is thy ransom. It is the last of my treasures which I kept for the King."

While he spoke, a shuddering earthquake rocked the city, and the sky grew dark. A heavy roof tile fell and struck the old man on the temple. The girl bent over him. She heard a voice come through the twilight, like music from a distance. The girl turned to see if someone had spoken from the window above them, but she saw no one.

Then the old man's lips began to move as if in answer: "Not so, my Lord. For when did I see Thee hungry and feed Thee? Or thirsty, and give Thee drink? When did I see Thee a stranger, and take Thee in? Or naked, and clothe Thee? When did I see Thee sick or in prison, and come unto Thee? Three-and-thirty years have I looked for Thee; but I have never seen thy face, nor ministered to Thee, my King."

He ceased, and the sweet voice came again. And again the maid heard it, very faintly and far away. But now it seemed as though

26

she understood the words: "Verily I say unto thee, inasmuch as thou hast done it unto one of the least of these my brethren, thou hast done it unto me."

A calm radiance of wonder and joy lighted the pale face of Artaban like the first ray of dawn on a snowy mountain peak. One long, last breath of relief exhaled gently from his lips. His journey was ended. His treasures were accepted. Artaban had found the King.

May you, like Artaban, find your life to be a precious gift for the King. Amen.

1998

Living in an Open Circle
EPHESIANS 2:11-22

Rev. Martin C. Singley III
Tellico Village Community Church
Loudon, Tennessee

Sandy and I were riding down the hotel elevator in Columbus, Ohio, this week. Next to us stood a short, cute woman named Suzy. Suzy was a delegate to our Community Church Conference. And she was excited. You see, Suzy is an Eskimo woman from Wassail, Alaska. And on Wednesday night, Suzy experienced a thunderstorm for the first time in her life! She'd never before seen lightning, or heard the rumble of thunder. She thought it was *wonderful*! In fact, the children who were also in her delegation stood by the window of their fourteenth floor hotel room, absolutely mesmerized by nature's fireworks! The circle of their life experience was stretched to include this exciting new discovery.

Suzy and the children were members of the Majestic Mountain Community Church in Wasilla. They describe their church as an *inclusive* Christian fellowship that is ecumenical, interracial, and intercultural. It is a church that spreads its arms to reach *everyone*. In much the same way that Suzy and the kids found the circle of their experience stretching to include a good old midwestern thunderstorm, the Majestic Mountain Community Church *itself* lives as an open circle of God's amazing grace.

And that's what I want to chat with you about – *living in an open circle*. But first, let me tell you about the great toilet paper caper.

Nothing I ever learned in Seminary prepared me for what I encountered in the very first church I pastored all by myself. I was at the Annual Meeting, and we were dealing with some very important issues about the church's ministry and mission. There was a healthy debate about how our work would be funded for the coming year, and a detailed analysis of what had happened in the year gone by. Somewhere in the course of looking ahead and reflecting backwards, though, someone spotted it in the Treasurer's report. It was a line item under the Trustees budget: *Toilet paper - $49.99.*

Now this was a small church with a small budget. $49.99 was a lot of money! And $49.99 back in those days bought a lot of toilet paper. Someone said to the chair of the Trustees, *"Jack, why in the world did you spend $49.99 on toilet paper?"* Jack turned about four different shades of red, and then blurted out, *"I DIDN'T buy $49.99 worth of toilet paper... but I'd like to get my hands on who did!"*

There was a rumbling and a grumbling among the people, and fingers were pointed at each other. Everybody had a theory about who it was who bought the paper, and being New Englanders at an annual meeting in the dead-cold middle of winter, they didn't hesitate to heat things up by publicly accusing each other of being the culprit.

"When I get my hands on whoever did this without the authority of the Board," Jack bellowed, *"I'll..."* But Jack never finished the sentence. He stopped short when a small voice chirped, *"I did it. I bought the paper. I saw it on sale – 2 for 1 – and I thought in the long run it would save the church some money,"* said....Jack's...*wife!*

We never did make any important decisions that year about our ministry and mission. But we did pass a resolution saying that anyone who wanted to buy toilet paper for the church should check first with the Board of Trustees, or be prepared to pay for it themselves. Funny what we fight about in church! Often, it's silly stuff – like the great toilet paper caper. Or what color should we paint the front door?

But sometimes our fights are much more important. Do you know what the very first major fight was about in the New Testament Christian Church? It was a monumental battle about whether the church should be a *closed* circle, or an *open* circle. In a sense, it was a struggle about whether Christianity would be a *denominational* or a *community* church!

You see, our Community Church movement flows from a struggle that goes back to the very beginning of Christendom. On the one side was Peter and the Jerusalem Church. They adamantly argued that the Gospel was for those already inside the circle. God's promises were for Jews only. The role of the church was to take care of those inside it! But on the other side was St. Paul who insisted that the circle must be opened – to *everyone*! And the fledging Gentile congregations in Ephesus and Corinth and Galatia stood with Paul, for they had come to know Christ by way of those who believed the Church must be an *open* circle. And thank the Lord, Paul's side won that argument, because less than forty years later, that Jerusalem church died, as closed circles always do. The Gospel came to *us* through those churches planted by Paul. They were churches taught to be *open* circles of God's amazing grace.

Our reading from the second chapter of Ephesians tells us that the death of Christ on the Cross requires us to live in an open circle. The Cross upon which the Savior died has been placed in the very center of all the little circles in which we live, and in His death, the dividing walls have all been flattened.

Now, *we are to step into each other's lives, learn to love one another in Christ, and work together to bring Christ's healing to the world*. Are you willing to live in an open circle? You shouldn't answer that question too quickly. Most of us don't really fathom what it involves to live in an *open* circle. In fact, what many of us think are the open circles of our lives are not really *open* circles at all, but rather simple extensions of closed circles.

For instance, I can tell you honestly that it's easy for me to relate comfortably with the International Council of Community Churches. We are the most racially inclusive religious body in North America and probably the world. Half our churches are comprised of primarily Caucasian members, and half have mainly African-American members. Our annual Conferences are exhilarating celebrations of a diverse Christian community with many kinds of music and preaching and worship.

What a thrill it is for some of us white ministers to preach sermons that the congregation actually helps you with! *Amen! Yes, Lord! Ah, hah! Thank you, Jesus!* Preaching is a *team sport* in black churches! In fact, if you're making a really good point, and the

African-American congregation is with you, they'll sometimes holler, *"Take your time!"* They don't worry about tee times or brunch at the Yacht Club. You can go two, three hours if you're hot. *Take your time!* But, if you're standing up there preaching a real dud, someone – sooner or later – will call out, *"Step it up!"* – which is simply a polite was of saying, *"You lost us a long time ago, so why don't you just stop now, so maybe we can go and GET a tee time!"*

Now, it's easy for me to be a part of this kind of experience because my life was formed and nurtured during the Civil Rights Movement. My pastor, George Seale, was a Civil Rights activist. In fact, Reverend Seale once rented an apartment he owned to a black family and some of the neighbors wanted to lynch him. They harassed the black family, hoping they'd move away. When my parents found out about this, they threw the three of us kids into the car and down to the apartment. We drove to greet the family, and offer them a housewarming gift, and to spend an evening enjoying each other's company as friends. I guess it was also to symbolize to our white friends that if they messed with the Hazzards, they messed with the Singley's, too.

My life circle has, from the earliest years, included close relationships with African-Americans. But last Friday night, I discovered that, though, the circle may be wide, *it isn't really as open as I thought*. Dr. Greg Smith, our new Council President was preaching. Greg is someone I deeply love and respect. He preached a marvelous message about how openness to each other creates struggle – because we are different, because we see and experience things differently. He said the struggle is painful; it is fraught with difficulty. But it is *out of this struggle of the open circle that God brings blessing! It has always been so!*

That really inspired me – until Greg spoke about the apology. Do you know what I'm talking about? There is discussion in the land today about whether or not the government of the United States of America ought to offer an apology to African-Americans for its complicity in the human slavery that existed prior to the Civil War. Smith was very impassioned about this. He reminded us of the fact that we have apologized to Japanese Americans interred during World

31

War II, and the Native Americans whose lands were unjustly taken, and that we have even rebuilt at great cost the countries of those who have attacked us in war. And yet, Greg Smith intoned, there are many who believe that an apology to African-Americans in not needed. Believe me, none of the black delegates were telling Greg Smith to *step it up*. They were right with him, team-preaching the point with great passion.

I found myself in a strange place. For all the connection I have had with African-Americans from my youngest years, for all the openness I *thought* I had, I found myself very closed and disconnected to what Greg was saying. I wondered why Greg needed to clutter up a really great sermon with this apology business. Well, after reflecting upon this over the past forty-eight hours, I now realize that I was listening to Greg Smith from within my own circle, through the walls of my own experience as a middle-class white person. I was hearing him through the walls of my political orientation which runs toward the wall of my own lifetime of interracial experience which I had thought was pretty tolerant and empathetic toward blacks, and really had nothing to apologize for.

I guess what I did was to hear Greg through the thick walls that still surround the circle of my life no matter how *wide* I might think that circle to be. But what I did *not* do was to hear Greg's words from within *his* circle, from behind *his* eyes, from within *his* experience. Might life look a little bit different if you see it from within the heart of another?

That's what it means to live in an *open* circle. It is open not so much to let others in as it is to let you *out*! It is not to stretch out *your* world, but to *step into another's world.* You see, that's the Jesus story! The Word became flesh and dwelt among us! The sacred became the secular. The divine became human! God became one of us! God stepped out of His own circle, and took up residence within *our* circle. He saw what we see, he heard what *we* hear, he experienced *our* pain, and he *took it upon himself!* And, in so doing, Ephesians tells us, Jesus died! That's what happens when you live in an open circle. You die with Christ to the smallness of your life, and you are raised with

Christ into a daring new creation that becomes *redemptive* to others when you step into *their* circle and learn to love from there.

I'm not sure I agree with Greg about the apology, but I'm now trying to understand why he feels about it as he does. Living in an open circle does *not* mean we buy into everybody else's viewpoints and behaviors. It means we commit ourselves to loving others no matter what, and out of that love seeking to understand them.

I love the story about the grandfather whose 14-year old grandson came to visit. They were riding along in the grandfather's big Buick when the grandfather said, *"Timmy, why don't we put on some music."* He reached into his shirt pocket and pulled out a tape. It was rap music! Timmy looked incredulously at his grandpa. *"You sure you want to listen to this, Grandpa?"* *"Of course,"* his grandfather said. *"I don't understand all the words, but I really like the beat."* So Timmy, with a smile, put in the tape and down the road they went, that big Buick putting out the pulsing bass notes like a loudspeaker on wheels.

Later, Timmy's grandfather, in the privacy of his own bathroom, swallowed three or four Excedrin tablets. Living in an open circle is not as easy as it sounds. But it is where God brings people together. I have a lot of work to do in opening up the circle of my life. I hope you'll work at it, too.

1999

CHILDREN OF THE SAME GOD
GALATIANS 3:23-29

Rev. Herbert Freitag, Pastor
Chapel By The Sea
Clearwater Beach, FL.

An exciting week lies ahead for our church. Beginning tomorrow, this year's the annual conference of the International Council of Community Churches will be held at the Hilton Hotel on Clearwater Beach! About 600 people will be coming here from all over the country; from all over the world! And despite their similarities, they will exhibit many differences - differences in terms of background, experiences, traditions, age, sex, color. Now, at and during this conference we are going to celebrate our commonness and our diversity! And we can do that because we are open and accepting people... despite our differences.

However, this conference will not reflect the world as we usually experience it - the "real" world. Regarding our Council churches ... approximately half are white and half are black. Regarding our conference attendees... approximately half are white and half are black. For those of us who have been part of this organization and coming to this conference for some time, this is one of its attributes and opportunities which we know and love. But for new-comers... well, it might take some getting used to!

Have you ever heard anyone say: "I don't see color!" Of course you have. What baloney! I think I know where they are coming from. Their intentions are good; their hearts are right... but the statement is still baloney! And frequently such an

34

observation is made by someone who is desperate to be and/or appear tolerant and unprejudiced. Nonetheless, it doesn't make sense. And it is completely impossible. Additionally, carried to its logical conclusion, the view is demeaning and counter-productive. Because, you see, if it were true, it would take away one of the very things which makes and identifies the whole and total person!

Let me carry that last thought to an extreme. Suppose one could get to the point where he or she really did not see color. Does that mean that he or she would also not see sex or age or size, etc.? If I were blind to all those characteristics of a person, it could get very confusing. Let me illustrate. I know this is my friend, Anthony Wells. There are certain things about him which help me in the identification. But if I did not see color, sex, age, size, I might think this was a twenty year-old, 120 pound, 6'7", blond-haired and blue-eyed member of the professional Swedish women's basketball team! And then I could not possibly ascertain anything about Anthony which would help me really know and understand him!

As with age and sex, and size, race contributes to making us what we are; to making us what we become. And it gives us clues about each other. As a white man, I cannot even pretend to "feel" or "know" the black experience. Perhaps I can somewhat understand intellectually certain and limited aspects and elements of it...somewhat ... but I have not been through it! So, my comprehension could never be complete.

One of my clergy friends in Ohio was Harold Turner. Harold is black. Harold and I were rather close. We went through some ups and downs together. We watched each other's kids grow up. We shared ideas and observations, hopes and dreams. About 25 years ago, Harold and I were driving together to a minister's seminar just outside of Buffalo, New York. Twelve noon arrived, and we began to consider stopping for lunch. Ahead was a diner with a bunch of trucks in its parking lot. Well, you know what they say about restaurants with trucks - if the truckers go there, the food has to be pretty good. We pulled in. After eating and again "hitting the road", Harold mentioned to me that if we had not been together, he would never have gone there! I was caught off guard... but I soon understood what he was talking about. And then, as the conversation continued, I heard about earlier times when he and Vera, if and when they traveled with their family, always took along food and drink just in case they could not find a place where it was comfortable and safe to stop! That was not the kind of thing I had ever had to think about; that was not the kind of thing I had ever had to worry about! I had also never had to think or worry about being refused service at a lunch counter; about being sent to the back of the bus; about not being rented a hotel or motel room; about having to use separate and unequal rest rooms; about being attacked because of a particular ethnicity! Such concerns were simply not part of my experience!

My friends, there are already enough built-in handicaps which prevent us from more fully understanding each other. So we don't have to add yet one more by refusing to "see" and acknowledge another person's race or color. Indeed, it is a vital and revealing part of that individual's history and development and "totality"! If l don't see your color. .. then I don't see all of you. If l don't see your color... then you, for me, are less than complete. If l don't see your color... then I have little or no idea where you are coming from. If l don't see your color... then I have stripped you of part of what makes you, you!

So what does color (like age or sex and so on) tell us about others? Well, it certainly does not give us the whole story. There are always parts of every person which no other person can ever completely know or understand. But even if I cannot empathize with you because I haven't experienced what you have experienced ... when I see as much of the whole you as possible: I can get an idea of the battles you've fought and the goals you've sought and the disappointments you've endured and the obstacles you've overcome and the dreams you've had and the victories you've won; I can get an idea of some of what has gone into the formation of your character and your personality; I can get an idea of where you might be coming from on given issues and concerns. And I can also try to better understand your feelings as you live life in your particular portion of our common world!

So, I don't want to hear anyone say: "I don't see color!" Because, I won't believe them. But what I do want to hear is: "I do see color... but it doesn't matter!" It doesn't matter in the sense that it doesn't stand **in** the way of mutual understanding and relationship, of mutual acceptance and respect!

Paul talked about Christianity eradicating the importance of differences. He said that faith in God through Christ makes us family. He mentioned that, therefore, there were (within the Christian fold) no longer Jew or Greek, slave or free, male or female. But Paul was talking about this being true within the context of the church. When folks returned to the world outside the church... the old "rules" still applied! Well, let me suggest to you that one of the true ends or goals of Christianity is to do away with the importance of such differences throughout the world ... and not just within the Christian community! Our aim ought to be to have all people accept one another as brothers and sisters... despite their differences!

One thing which is so special about any ICCC conference is that at it we get to meet others as people; as individuals. And in such a setting we cannot hide behind the possession of group stereotypes and prejudices. A conference further offers us the opportunity to be completely and refreshingly honest. You know, that's one thing which is still sometimes lacking among us - real honesty. We are so busy being nice, we are not always really honest! And without honesty, we can go just so far on niceness! If we cannot be honest with one another without risking ruptures in relationships, then we still have a considerable way to go! I suggest that we can be honest without being rude or disrespectful... just like we can disagree without being disagreeable.

Let me tell you a secret. There are some black folks I'm not crazy about. Of course, there are even more white folks I'm not crazy about. But all that has nothing to do with whether they're black or white. Rather, it has to do with how we get along as people; how we relate to one another - as fellow human beings! We need to get ourselves to the place where we do not accept or reject others because of race. Instead, we should respect one another as particular and unique persons - in openness; in honesty; in acceptance! We're not all the same... and yet... we are all the same! Do you understand what I'm trying to say? We are all different... and our differences help make us what we are - special and unique. Yet we are all people - part of the same family!

When I moved to Clearwater Beach in 1981, I had a good friend in Detroit, Michigan. Tragically, Dareau Stewart (a black man, a black minister) died about a month after I arrived. I still miss him. I think that ours was a unique relationship. I believe that we both benefited from it. He said things to me which I doubt he ever said to any other white man. And I know I said things to him which I never said to any other black man. And we could do that because we had "paid our dues"! We had gone through some highs and lows together. We had fought some fights together. We had talked and argued and disagreed with one another. And we had earned each other's trust; each other's respect; each other's love! Darneau and I realized and valued each other's differences! They helped make us what we were - people to be cared about by the other.

Here's a real shocker which you are going to have difficulty accepting - everyone doesn't like me! Now don't "pish-tush" - it's true. I, too, find it hard to understand... but there you have it. And yet even my staunchest critics will admit that I'm up-front and outspoken - they always know exactly where I'm coming from. Earlier I said that what I don't want to hear is: "I don't see color!" And then I went on to suggest that what we should hope for is the ability to honestly say: "I do see color. .. but it doesn't matter!" That would be the ideal. But now let me observe that the best I think we can currently and truly offer is: "I do see color... but I don't want it to matter!" That means we're trying; we're working; we're striving! That means that as people (black and white) of good will... we want to make a difference; we want things to drastically change! That means we are recognizing our weaknesses and prejudices (and we all have them)... but we're doing something about them!

My friends, unless and until we accept people as people... this world won't change. And what's holding us back besides our stubbornness, our anger, our pride, our fear? We may be different... but we are all children of the same God! And that makes us family.

2000

A Single Point of Difference
EPHESIANS 4:1-7, GALATIANS 3:28, JOHN 17:21

Rev. David H. Blanchett
Majestic Mountain Community Church
Wasilla, Alaska

I was watching President Bill Clinton this January give his State of the Union address. Somewhere among his requests for the support of programs that he felt all Americans should rally around, he made what I thought was an interesting remark. He said that a most learned and noted genetic scientist had explained to his wife that human beings, no matter where they live on this planet, "are genetically, ninety-nine point nine percent the same." Modern science affirms what ancient faith has always taught: The most important fact of life is our common humanity. Therefore, we must do more than tolerate diversity – we must honor it and celebrate it." To a hushed audience, President Clinton continued – "Some of you here might have a problem with that."

Some of us do. We have a problem. We have a problem because we dwell on the single point of difference and not on the ninety-nine points of similarity. We have a problem because we look negatively on the point of difference. We have a problem because we try to justify the point of difference as a liability, a curse, or something to be ashamed of or not to be around. When in fact we should be witnesses that the point of difference is a blessing and a gift from God. A point of difference is given to each person. Why? Do we not know that the point of difference another has, is our treasure too – a treasure to be lifted up to give glory to God?

Since we are so much alike, what is the meaning of the point of difference? Let me propose that it is our identity. Isn't it great that we don't have to see people who are exact copies of ourselves every where we go? What we see are all manner of race, shape, size, and

41

cultures! All people made in the image of God – special in God's sight!

Jesus prayed that we all be one, as he and the Father are one. Jesus' desire is not only that all would be saved, but also that we be in unity with each other and God. In unity, we must let people be who they are. Let people retain their gift of culture. Let people use and share their unique gifts that God has given to the church through them.

Too often a local church cries out for people who are different to come and join our communion! But they only really accept them if they change to be like everyone else in the congregation – check their culture at the door. We must not be so insensitive!

An Alaskan Native was wooed into a particular mainline church that was encouraging Eskimos to join. The following week at the church potluck, not one person touched or sampled the traditional dish this new member worked so diligently to bring and share with those who were different.

Paul and all the other "big boys" and saintly sisters in the New Testament, did not strip people of their culture or ridicule their gifts. They preached Jesus, sinless, crucified, and resurrected. They expounded on the unity we should have with each other so that united we can lift each other and go forth to spread the good news that Jesus saves, and he saves to the utmost. That point of difference is not something to divide us but to be a catalyst and adhesive to keep us marveling at God's work and love! Marveling at the work of God in the land and giving testimony and praise!

Diversity in God's church must not cause division. We can experience unity without uniformity. We must practice dialogue free of dictation. If together we walk in the light in unity, it will be oh so victorious!

It was the summer of 1994 and I was in Marlborough, Massachusetts for my first conference of the International Council of Community Churches. Our small Alaskan church in Wasilla had just affiliated with the International Council of Community Churches. At the first meeting I attended in a grand auditorium of the hotel, I looked out at the hundreds of people present. Gazing at such a sea of

42

people, you would expect to see all the Blacks sitting together over here and all the Whites sitting together over there. And in addition you would also expect that within those racial groups, there would be further division, a segregation of male and female.

What I saw was a mixed multitude. A sea of race and sex so scattered, it was as if someone had taken a giant spoon and stirred this mixture of flesh so that they indeed looked totally united! Also to my surprise, the mixture also included persuasions of Methodist, Presbyterian, Baptist, Pentecostal, Catholic, you name it. They were together freely and joyfully worshipping and praising Jesus the Christ!

Is this what Jesus meant about Unity? You bet! Are we perfect in our endeavors? No. But we will keep striving! Why? Because doing the will of God allows us to live victorious here on earth, not in confusion, not in mistrust, not in ignorance, but in love!

Reverend Martha Blanchett, the first Eskimo ordained in the African Methodist Episcopal Zion Church said: "There is no Baptist heaven, no Moravian heaven, no Methodist heaven, no denominational heaven, but just heaven. A heaven for any and all who accept God's gift of eternal life." Let us always cheerfully, prayerfully, praisefully unite in Christ – interculturally, interracially and ecumenically, in spirit and in truth!

2001

One Baptism (Yes, Just One!)
EPHESIANS 4:1-6

Rev. Robert Fread
Kawkawlin Community Church
Kawkawlin, Michigan

I am not sure how many times someone has said to me, "I'm a baptized Lutheran," or "I'm a baptized Catholic," or "I'm a baptized Presbyterian" or some sentence very similar. Yet every time I hear this I want to yell... "No, no, no!! You ARE NOT a baptized Lutheran, Catholic or Presbyterian. You ARE a baptized Christian!" I will grant that a person may have been baptized in a Lutheran church, or using a Roman Catholic liturgy, or been raised within the Presbyterian tradition. But there is just one Baptism. True, the age of the candidates may vary, the type of church may vary, the liturgy may vary, even the amount of water may vary, but there is just one Baptism and that is baptism into Christ!

The early Church used a variety of models and images for Baptism. The Scriptures give witness to this variety as it speaks of Baptism as... being joined to Christ's death and resurrection (Romans 6:3-5 & Colossians 2:12),...a salvation experience (I Peter 3:21),...a re-clothing in Christ (Galatians 3:27),...a liberation into a new humanity (Galatians 3:28),...a forgiveness of sin (Acts 2:38), and an entrance into one body by one spirit (I Corinthians 12:13). Even though the models and images vary greatly, each gives witness to a different facet of just one reality – one Baptism. As Ephesians puts it, "There is one body and one spirit, just as you were called to one hope of your calling, one Lord, one faith, one baptism." (Ephesians 4:4-5) That's right, one Baptism, yes, just one.

As a Community Church we seek to give an inclusive and ecumenical witness to the one Baptism. As a congregation we have chosen to make our baptismal practices as varied as the whole Christian family which is called Church. We allow individuals and families according to their faith and tradition to determine the appropriate age for Baptism – for some of us believe that children may and should be baptized, while others of us believe that only persons who can personally profess faith should be baptized. We baptize people in both categories, yet there is just one Baptism. We allow individuals and families to choose the mode of baptism – for some of us believe that Baptism must be by immersion in water, while others of us believe that pouring water over a person's head is also appropriate. In this Community Church we baptize persons both ways, yet there is just one Baptism!

In 1996 I was appointed to chair a committee whose mission was to develop the opening worship celebration for the Michigan Ecumenical Forum's annual assembly. The assembly theme was "One Lord, One Faith, One Baptism" and the worship service was to be a service of baptismal renewal in celebration of our common Baptism. The challenge of this endeavor is that the Michigan Ecumenical Forum (MEF) is an organization composed of 29 denominations/ communions and 15 ecumenical organizations from around the state. Not only were the usual ecumenical churches involved in the MEF – Presbyterian, Methodist, United, Disciples, Episcopal, Lutheran – but also churches such as Brethren, Moravian, Baptist, Roman Catholic, Christian Science, Reorganized Latter Day Saints, and Russian Orthodox. With that type of diversity, how could this committee be inclusive to all? We decided to not gloss over our diversity but to take it seriously. We went back to ideas learned in Theology 101 that Christians tend to have three different views on Baptism. Some see Baptism as a sacrament which means it is a visible sign that conveys God's invisible grace. Others accept Baptism as an ordinance meaning that it is a human response of discipleship. Lastly, some view Baptism as spiritual so that water is not used, but it is the Holy Spirit's activity in a person that is important. Then we invited three speakers, one to represent each view – an Episcopal bishop to give the sacramental view, a district minister of the Church of Brethren to give the ordinance view, and a captain from the Salvation Army to give the spiritual view. Surprisingly, the highly sacramental person that I am, found great areas of agreement with the two that didn't represent my belief. Just one more testimony to me that there is just one Baptism. Finally, as that service concluded we invited everyone to come forward to a large bowl of water and form one body, yet told the people to let their beliefs on Baptism dictate their actions. Some people dipped their fingers in the water and made the sign of the cross, some splashed water on their faces, some touched the bowl but not the water, while some ignored the water and greeted their sisters and brothers in Christ. This mass of humanity was a beautiful sign of how our one Baptism, even understood differently, makes us one body in Christ.

These same diverse views on Baptism are present in our Community Church movement every day. Yet it is just one Baptism that unites us. In January, 2002, our International Council of Community Churches will join eight other church bodies in a new relationship known as Churches Uniting in Christ (CUIC). One of the marks of this new relationship is that all the churches in CUIC will recognize the members of the other churches in one Baptism. Truly we will share one Baptism into one body by one Spirit, as together we declare to the whole world that there is one Lord, one faith, and one God of all.

As a Community Church we not only preach about "one Baptism", but we try to practice what we preach. That is why every year we join with other churches in an ecumenical celebration of Baptism. Every Easter our congregation joins with sisters and brothers in Christ from Westminster Presbyterian, Messiah Lutheran, and First Congregational United Church of Christ to celebrate the sacraments of Baptism and Holy communion. If you have never attended this service, this is what you have missed. Each year one of the four pastors is selected as a presider and leads the baptismal portion of the service, including questioning the candidates. Then the pastor of each church baptizes the candidates from his/her own church. Finally the pastors as a group lay hands upon each of the newly baptized. The ancient sign of bestowing the Holy Spirit (Acts 8:17) is also a confirmation that the baptism of one church is truly the baptism of all churches. Both Sara and Hanna (my children) were baptized at Easter in this very ecumenical and unique way. Sara was baptized by the Presbyterian pastor at the Lutheran church by having water poured over her head. Hanna was baptized by the United Church of Christ pastor, here in our Community church by being immersed in the water. Both children following their baptism had hands laid on them by the Presbyterian, Lutheran, and UCC Pastors, as well as myself. With such ecumenical baptisms I've almost guaranteed that the only statement my children can ever make is "I'm a baptized Christian!" Truly, every Easter we witness to the fact, there is just one Baptism.

As a Community Church we are a diverse people committed to unity in Christ. In our diversity we may baptize different people, in different ways, with different views, but all are baptized: in one Lord, by one Spirit, into one body, through one faith, by one Baptism, yes, just one!

2002

Tragedy and God's Will
GENESIS 50:15-21

Dr. C. David Matthews
Good Samaritan Church
Orlando, Florida

You remember Joseph. The favorite son. The boy with the coat of many colors, who was so intimidating to his brothers. Joseph the dreamer. A boy who dreams that much, and talks about it that much, has to be a problem to his siblings.

One day his brothers hit upon the idea of selling him to a passing caravan. Maybe you've had similar thoughts about your relatives! Years later a famine strikes, and the brothers have to go to Egypt to plead for food. Little do they know that the high Egyptian official to whom they are speaking is their brother, whom they sold many years before into slavery.

He toys with them a while, then reveals himself. *"I am Joseph."* They are shocked and become anxious, as you can imagine. He tells them to not be afraid. He says that, despite all the evil they intended, God has been strangely at work.

The summer of 1973 was the last of the summers I spent writing my doctoral dissertation. I worked in a tiny cubicle in the library of Southwestern Seminary. In that small space was a large, very old desk, and an ancient revolving bookcase. Generations earlier, the desk had belonged to B.H. Carroll, an early president of the seminary. A bit more recently, but still long ago, the revolving bookcase had belonged to a former pastor of the church I was at that time pastoring, Dr. Jeff Ray, who had come to the seminary to teach preaching. I sat between the desk and the bookcase that summer and wrote 200 pages on the providence of God.

I had decided before I began my graduate studies that I wanted to do my dissertation on providence. Throughout the twentieth

48

century it was the most neglected of the classical Christian doctrines, yet it was the very place where so much of the water hit the wheel for me.

What does it matter what God has done, or what God will do, if we cannot talk about what God is doing now? How much does it matter how active God was in the history of Israel and the early church, if we cannot believe that God is actively involved in everyone's history...in all of history? So, that was a summer more than any other dedicated to understanding providence.

Yet it was a summer intermittently interrupted by bad news. I had trouble working on divine providence because of human tragedy.

At the first part of the summer I had to leave my cubicle because a seminary faculty member, the father of one of the student members of my church, died of a heart attack. There was the evening I was working late, alone, with my whole family in Denver, and my work was interrupted by a long distance call that my mother had been hospitalized with cancer. I couldn't work anymore that night. There was the evening, a Wednesday evening, I was tying up loose ends for the rest of the week at church so I could return to the seminary. Suddenly the word came that one of our best, a bright piece of the future, had been killed less than an hour earlier in a senseless automobile accident. There was the morning when my clock radio awakened me in the dorm room I was renting with two horrifying items of news. One had to do with mass murder, perversion and sadism beyond belief; the other was about a small child apparently trapped in a car somewhere in New Mexico with the body of his dead father, crying for help over a C.B. radio.

We, the people who affirm the providence of a gracious God, have so many days when the word *"providence"* sounds like a cruel joke, and we want to cry, *"My God, my God, why have you forsaken us!"*

This is one of the very oldest philosophical questions. *"Whence comes evil?" "Why is there so much suffering in the world?"*

49

The church has been so concerned to preserve the belief that God is in control of the world that it has rushed in with quick answers. Too often they have been inadequate and even unfortunate answers.

We have been told, for example, that when tragedy comes we are to say, *"This is what is best."* We need to be careful with the words, *"All things work together for good."* First, this is not the most accurate translation of Romans 8; and, second, as I heard a Christian doctor say, it just won't sell at places like M.D. Anderson. There are plenty of situations that do not turn out good for anybody.

We have been told, *"Tragic things happen to teach us something, to make us stronger, or more faithful, or more courageous."* People say, *"God won't let anymore come to me than I can bear."* This comes, not from a bad translation, but from a simple misreading of Scripture. That isn't in the Bible. Look around. Lots of people have more dumped on them than they can carry. If that were not true, there would be no such thing as suicide.

We have been told, *"Tragic things happen because God is punishing us for something."* Now, you may think you know better, but there is something innate in all of us that causes us to feel that way. You get a punch in the midsection, and as you go to your knees and gasp for breath you almost automatically ask, *"What have I done to deserve this?"* It's an ancient religious conviction that evil and suffering are God's way of punishing sin. But the Bible says the rain falls on the just and the unjust alike.

I must tell you that, between the heavy, scarred desk and the funny, old bookcase, I found no glib and easy answers, no smooth and satisfying solutions, to the *"Why?"* of human tragedy. I warn you, in a week such as this, to beware of simple answers. If our Christian faith is not to be a pious escapism, then there are some things we need to be honest about.

These things seem to me to be true:

1. Much tragedy comes simply as a result of statistical probability.

The created world is – to a large degree – predictable. Things usually react in expected ways. Of course we are not locked in a world of Iron Law, as science is discovering today. But things generally follow predictable patterns of reaction.

Spong says that one of God's gifts is contained in the fact that, if you put your eye in front of a line drive, you will lose your eye. Or, take penicillin. Most are healed by it. But some are so allergic to it that it can kill them. Is it the will of God in both cases? I don't think so...not directly. It is the result of statistical probability.

Here is one child with leukemia in a room full of healthy children. Here is a man who dies of a stroke long before he has reached the average person's life expectancy. Here is a woman who – in the prime of a useful life – develops a mysterious malignancy. Here is one house in a block of houses that is destroyed by a tornado. This young man was killed in the collapse of Tower 1, while another was, fortunately, late for work. The will of God? What kind of God? More likely, the result of statistical probability.

2) Much tragedy comes as a result of human limitations.

Given the charge to be the caretakers of the earth, we have taken giant strides in developing the world's potential, but we have not yet mastered creation. In some ways we are still quite primitive, even as we continue to discover the earth's resources and harness them for good.

Fifty years ago the cancer patient was told, *"We can give you morphine for pain, but there is no drug to cure your malignancy."* Twenty-five years ago the cancer patient was told, *"There is a drug available that has produced some tumor shrinkage in some patients. We will try it with you."* Today the cancer patient is told: *"We will treat you with chemicals and other agents. There is a chance of long-term control of the disease. A remission of five years, which now comes in a majority of cases, will mean that we can cure you of cancer.*"

Some of us remember those days when so many lives were permanently marred by polio. Because of the Salk vaccine, that will never be true again. Some tragedy is the result of human limitation.

3) Some tragedy is the result of human irresponsibility and wickedness.

Has there ever been a more vivid demonstration of this than what happened in this nation on Tuesday? I think I am a mature adult, but I am continually shocked by the human capacity for evil. Do not tell me that demonic powers are not at work in our world through the souls of human beings.

It is not just the horrors of this past Tuesday, as you well know. The media bring to us daily endless accounts of outrageous cruelty. We constantly witness the suffering of children and other innocents at the hands of incomprehensible evil. Much tragedy results from the dark side of the human heart and the deadly misuse of human freedom.

We must be honest and realistic about these things, I think. Tragedy comes through statistical probability, human limitations, and simple wickedness.

How, then, can we speak of providence? What has all of this to do with the will of God?

In my little cubicle that summer, I was thrown back time after time from the eloquent words and elaborate systems of the theologians, which may not help much when the crisis comes, no matter how profound they are, to the only answer God seems to have given. The cross.

It seems to me that none of the traditional answers to our *"Why?"* questions take the cross into consideration. We have never liked having to look at the cross. But it won't be dismissed, and cannot be explained away. We think it somehow represents what God wanted all along. The cross, however, is what God did ***not*** want, but chose anyway.

The cross tells me that God honors human freedom. It says that God allows statistical probability, our limitations, and our wickedness. There is no freedom if these things are not real.

It also tells me, however, that in the very places where human freedom is abused, in the most tragic situations, the divine will is at work. God's will does not prevent tragedy, but transforms it. The cross becomes, not a symbol of tragedy, but the supreme symbol of victory. Death is transformed into life.

This is what Paul Tillich meant when he said that in every situation there is a *"saving possibility."* God's will means that the destructive power of evil can never have an unbreakable hold on us. This is what Karl Barth meant, when very old and seriously ill, in a personal letter he wrote saying that the "bacillus" might enter his kidneys, which would mean his end, but that the "bacillus" could not destroy the kingdom of his God. This is what the apostle Paul meant when he claimed that nothing can separate us from the love of God. And I think this must be what Oscar Wilde meant when he wrote in *De Profundus, "Where there is tragedy, there is holy ground."*

Joseph stands before his brothers and says, *"You intended evil, but God turned it into good."* No, Joseph, statistical probability sent you to Egypt, human limitation, your brothers' wickedness. Joseph says to us: *"I have found the healing dimension of all this. I have seen that God is at work where God seems to be hidden."*

I have tried to point out this morning the crucial difference between speaking of what God *causes* and speaking of what God does not cause but *uses* in the service of love. I have wanted to speak of what Paul Scherer and Paul the Apostle call *"the pain God is allowed to guide."*

The late American theologian Nels Ferre has always been helpful to me in my musings on providence. A student of his came to resent his teacher's unrelenting emphasis on the love of God, which was the cornerstone of Ferre's theology. This student, you see, was daily going from a hospital in the city to the seminary, then back to the hospital. His little child was dying of leukemia. He would come from watching the child's agony and burn with hostility in the classroom as this idealistic, ivory-towered professor spoke of the love of God. It was all he could do to refrain from standing and challenging everything he was hearing.

On the night the child died, the student related later, the first person that came to him and his wife was Dr. Ferre. Putting his arms around the grieving couple, he elucidated his teaching on the love of God. He said, *"I have come tonight to say to you that God is hurting as much as you are."*

It is the God of the cross, this suffering God of love, who makes it possible for people of faith to utter out of some dark night and lonely valley their strange doxologies of praise…and hope.

2003

God is Good – Always
PSALM 107:1

Dr. C. George Fry
Fairfield Parish
Lancaster, Ohio

A Thanksgiving Sermon

Six years ago during spring break I took several students to a Christian leadership conference sponsored by Senator Dan Coats. There were people from about every campus in Indiana and from about every denominational persuasion. Of the many fabulous speakers, one stood out. A big black man, he was chaplain for the Indianapolis Colts. His Sunday sermon recounted many terrible things – born fatherless, raised poor, barely escaping prison, coming to Christ just in the nick of time. All listening had teared up. Then came his testimony: "I have learned that God is good – *always*." God is good – *always* We need to hear that. Why? Because the *times* are not always good.

Aesop knew that. He told a tale of two sisters, twins, named Joy and Sorrow. Always they quarreled as to "which one should have the preference." Unable to settle it, they went to King Minos. Minos tried everything to "make them agree and go hand in hand together as loving sisters." No success. Minos finally settled it this way. Joy and Sorrow were chained together and "forever" each of them "In turn should be perpetually treading upon the heel of the other."[1]

Oliver Goldsmith told the tale, drawing this moral, "good and ill fortune do as naturally succeed one another as day and night."[2]

That's how it is. The good and the bad, alternating, just like the left and the right or sunshine and showers. Old timers in the room are nodding. They remember. The "Boom" of the Twenties, the "Bust" of the Thirties, or "World War" in the Forties, "World Peace" in the Fifties, or "Reform" in the Sixties, "Reaction" in the Seventies.

Our Days are checkered. So how dare we say that "God is good – always?" Yes, I can thank God for prosperity but not for adversity. Let me address that issue today. For we are, in the words of the Communion Liturgy, "at all times, and in all places, (to) give thanks unto thee, O Lord, Holy Father..."[3]

A Time of Adversity

The hard part of the text first.

God is good always, *even in time of adversity.*

For some, 2002 was a hard year. It brought sickness and death, heartbreak and distress. As one student told me Monday, "I just want to get the damned thing over." That bad!

Larry would agree. You'd never guess he was eighty-two. Dapper and dashing, he still works as a lawyer. Every day. A devout Christian, Larry acts half his age. One Saturday evening I ran into Larry. "Reverend, do you drink?" he asked. I instantly knew he didn't mean Diet Pepsi. "Yes, sir," I replied, "I was ordained Lutheran, wasn't I?" We ended up in Kaufman's. Over a cocktail, the sad story unfolded. Larry's first wife had been a keeper – lovely, gracious, sagacious. They had forty years of bliss, then ten years of hell. "Alzheimer's," he explained. "I finally had to put her into a nursing home," he cried. Weeping, he added, "I'd go, every day to see her, and she'd ask, 'Who is that man?'" Mercifully she died. Our eighty-year old widower met a sixty-nine-year-old widow. Those two gray panthers staged Romeo and Juliet. Whirlwind courtship. Larry glowed as he described his Mary as a keeper – lovely, gracious, sagacious. Then the tears revealed the tears in his heart. "We were married only a year. She was the one who had the heart attack!" A long pause ended with this question. "George, why didn't I die, not her? Why does God make me go through being a widower twice? It isn't fair." No, it isn't. Life isn't fair. But God is good – always. Though he does not promote adversity, he permits it. C.S. Lewis, who lost his wife to cancer, wrote, "God whispers in our pleasures...but shouts in our pains." There is a severe mercy in adversity.

In part it is a *matter of teaching*. Through pain can come again. Robert Browning Hamilton put it this way:

> I walked a mile with Pleasure
> She chattered all the way
> But left me none the wiser
> For all she had to say.
>
> I walked a mile with Sorrow
> And ne'er a word said she
> But oh the things I learned from her
> When Sorrow walked with me.[4]

Hamilton's right. At noon I see only single sun, but at midnight several millions. Only in the darkness is the Big Dipper visible. Some lessons are taught exclusively in God's Night School. Thank him for adversity – for he is good, always.

In part it is a *matter of testing*. Do I appreciate a meal more when I am empty or full? Often joy delayed is pleasure enhanced. How much do you want something? Wait and see. Patrick Dennis lived five years through fifteen rejections before Auntie Mame was published. Irving Stone endured seventeen refusals before *Lust for Life* was printed. Pearl Buck experienced twelve returns before *The Good Earth* was accepted. But, as Jackie Gleason said, at the happy ending of a "Honeymooners" skit, "How sweet it is." Some lessons are learned only in a holding pattern, so thank him for adversity, for he is good, always.

In part it is a *matter of directing*. Sometimes dead ends give live options. The detour becomes the fast lane. Loyola became a saint, not a soldier – because of a broken leg. Elizabeth Browning became a poet, not a debutante – because of an injured spine. Lord Byron and Sir Walter Scott became authors – because of lameness. Franklin D. Roosevelt didn't walk to the White House, he wheeled himself there – four times – because of polio. Josiah Wedgewood turned to making china – because of a leg amputation. Blessed adversities. Without Paul's thorn would we have Romans or I Corinthians? The pure poetry of Paul's "Ode to Love" makes his pain eternally profitable.

Without a cross, Jesus would have been a major philosopher; but through it, he became the world's Savior. Some lessons are directional signals, seen only on the detour. Thank God for adversity, for he is good, always.

It is always a *matter of training*, in faith. Faith is trusting God. By it we live. By it we die. It is the only thing we can take with us. Not health, or wealth, or fame, or fortune, or friends, or even our family. Faith saves. And it is learned in the School of Adversity. Martin Rinkart knew that. He was a Lutheran pastor during the terrors of the Thirty Year's War. His town was sacked, once by the Austrians, twice by the Swedes. With poverty came pestilence. In 1637 Rinkart was burying forty or fifty parishioners a day; in all, 4,480 people, including his own wife. For many it was a descent into hell, but for Rinkart, a consent to faith. During those apocalyptic days, he wrote "Now Thank We All our God."

> O may this bounteous God
> Through all our life be near us,
> With ever joyful hearts
> And blessed peace to cheer us;
> And keep us in his grace,
> And guide us when perplexed,
> And free us from all ills
> In this world and the next.
> Amen.

God is good – always.

A Time of Prosperity

Now the easy part of the text. God is good always, even in times of prosperity.

For some, 2002 was a good year. It brought health and birth, happiness and success. As one student told me Tuesday, "I just wished the year could last forever." That good!

Norma could agree. She was a non-traditional student at Lutheran College. "Dr. Fry," she asked, "are you having lunch in the ptomaine palace?" She meant the college cafeteria. "I'll buy," she said. Normally, I don't let students pay; but, since Norma graduates in December, there is no way the tab for greasy pizza would qualify as a bribe. After some chit-chat about her commute, the weather, and a tuition hike, came the real reason for the meal deal. Norma just wanted to share her joy. Four years ago she was a problem, now she's a promise. Norma's husband took a hike, leaving her alone with two infants, one a baby five months along. She was marginalized by any measure, drifting from one minimum wage job to another. "I didn't want to be a "Welfare Queen," she said. "I was down and out, so I had to look up." Some Basic Baptist was starting to kick in. "I said, 'Jesus, help me get my high school equivalency.'" Long pause. "Got it, so I prayed, 'Jesus, make me a nurse.'" In spite of age, obstacles, handicaps and hardships, Norma made it. This December she will get her rose, her pin, her diploma, and walk from that platform into a whole new life. "God sure is good," Norma said, and I echoed, "Umm, hmm, always." "Life," she answered, "life is wonderful "What next, Norma?" I inquired. "Missions," she affirmed, "I'm gonna give something back to God."

"When life is successful, God whispers, 'since I am good to you, take some of what you have, and share it." That is the one great lesson of prosperity – charity. I call this the greatest joy of having – giving.

Paradox? Apparent contradiction? Perhaps. But the supreme happiness of securing is sharing. Never are we more Godlike than when we give to others. Then we are the Lord's partner in the business of providence.

I learned that on a Thanksgiving Sunday twelve years ago. It is "The Tale of Two Georges." Let's move from Amanda to Motown. Let's go from this small white meeting house on the hill to a large red sandstone church in the inner city.

I was interim minister in a historic downtown Detroit congregation. Fifteen minutes before the service, we'd unlock. In would come the members – commuters from the Points and beyond the Outerbelt. In would come the regulars – the homeless, wanting a warm place in which to wait until the soup kitchen across the street opened. During the sermon they dozed, hoping for coffee and cookies during the Fellowship Hour. After the cake munch, that bunch went next door for their free lunch.

Most of the regulars were familiar. Same faces, same stories, same smells, every Sunday. After a few weeks of this, I was on to the "con" and my "closed heart" kept my wallet full.

This Sunday one of the regulars was an irregular. I'd never seen him before. Different. Quiet. Actually tried to follow the service. Seemed ashamed of his situation. Slipped into the coffee hour, but kept pretty much to himself. Curiosity got the best of me. After chit-chatting my lawyer, banker and college professor, I turned to my stranger. His name? George. This George had a very different life from mine. He was black, I was white. He was from Alabama, I was from Ohio. He was poor, I was born middle class. I finished school, he didn't. I went to Ohio State, he went to the state pen. His half century on the planet was a total contrast to mine. I tried to make some sense out of his story. George just got out of prison. That's why we'd never seen him before. He'd spent the night, a very cold November night, in an unheated flophouse. That explained his body odor, for there was no running water. That George was as happy as this George to be in church – he was there for the warmth; I was there for the worship. He ate the cookies because he was starving; I because I was sociable. There is a difference. "What next, George?" I asked. He paused. "I want to go home," he finally replied. "Where's that?" I queried. "Marbury, Alabama," he answered. I guess I looked puzzled "Near Birmingham, sir," he explained. "So you're going there for the holidays?" I inquired. "No, reverend, no," he explained.

I sensed the pain. Seemed real. That was his dream, not his scheme. By then I realized all George had left in this world was his mom, a widow, way down in the Cotton Belt, who longed to see her prodigal son, just once more, before she went to be with Jesus. A mother's love is endless. George had no bus fare. Possibly he could ride the rails. Or hitch hike. Or maybe he could find some work, to get some money, to pay his way.

I don't know why I did it.

Was it because I was paid that Sunday? All that new money waiting to be spent? Was it because I had listened to my own sermon?

Was it temporary insanity born of the sentimentality of the season "Come, George," I said, "let's go."

We left the warmth of the big red sandstone church to walk through drab Detroit streets, livened a bit by some sputtering snow flakes. We came to the Greyhound Station, and then our silence stopped. George figured it out. "Can't let you do this, Reverend," he protested. "I'm a Baptist, not a Congregationalist." "Be quiet," I insisted, "I'm neither. I'm Lutheran."

I got him a ticket. We grabbed a meal at the Burger King. I waited till he got on board a Dixie bound bus. That black face was wet with tears. "I'll send you the money, Doc," he promised, "just as soon as I get it."

"Not on your life," I commanded, "use it to buy your momma a Christmas present."

As the bus pulled out, a November snow began to fall in earnest. "Looks like Thanksgiving," I thought, as I made my way back to the church.

When I got there I was given a royal razzing. "You've been snookered," I was informed. Just another chapter of an Ohio country boy being taken by a big city con artist. Even I began to wonder.

I had just about forgotten, when, a few days before Christmas, a letter came. Worst scrawl I had ever seen. Grammar: atrocious! Sentence structure? A wreck! But I wasn't grading this paper. I was reading it – with my heart. It was from George. Postmarked Marbury, Alabama. "Here safe," it said. "Got my mother a nice Christmas present – just like I promised." Then, "She thanks you, so do I. God bless you, brother. Have a Merry Christmas." God is good – always.

And never is God nearer, than when he let's us play God by doing good to others.

"O give thanks unto the Lord, for he is good, for his mercy endureth forever." Amen (Psalm 107:1AV)

61

2004

Receiving Into Our Heart
ROMANS 15:1-7

Dr. Jeffrey R. Newhall
Greendale People's Church
Worcester, Massachusetts

Please pray with me: *From the arrogance that thinks it knows all truth, God, deliver us. From the laziness that is content with half-truths, O God deliver us. From the fear that hides from new truth, O God, deliver us, so we may be free and truly live. Amen.*

My text is from the seventh verse of chapter 15 of Romans: "Accept one another, then, just as Christ has accepted you." It is the climatic verse in a long passage of some thirty verses, beginning with verse one of chapter 14, in which Paul has been urging that Christians live in unity and peace. Now that is a state to be desired in the church, and certainly a worthy dream, but is it possible? Paul believes it is and he believes the way to living in peace and unity is through acceptance. That is the unifying theme of this passage as he begins the fourteenth chapter with a call to acceptance – "Accept the person whose faith is weak" – and ends with his call to "Accept one another just as Christ accepted you."

Now the word translated here as acceptance is an interesting Greek word that scholars struggle to translate into English. In the NIV, it is translated as *acceptance*, in the KJV, it is written as *receive*, and in the NRSV, we read it as *welcome*. In those three words – *accept, receive, welcome* – the translators are trying to convey the idea of receiving someone into one's self, welcoming a person into your heart. It is the same word that Jesus uses in the fourteenth chapter of John's Gospel where he says, "Let not your hearts be trouble...I will come again and will receive you to myself..." (John

14:1, 3) Paul means that we are to accept and welcome others just as Jesus accepts and welcomes us.

There is just one other place that Paul uses this word acceptance and it is in his very personal letter – the only personal letter of Paul's that we have – to Philemon. The cause for the letter is a runaway servant or slave names Onesimus, who has befriended Paul while the apostle sits in prison in chains. Indeed, Paul calls him "my son." But Paul knows that Onesimus has run away from Philemon, and, more than that, he has a history with Philemon. We gather from the letter that Onesimus was a lazy employee and one who stole from his employer. Yes, Philemon certainly has reason to be angry with Onesimus and to distrust him and Paul admits to that, but Paul wants them to reconcile, to make peace, by Philemon, for love of Paul, accepting and receiving into his heart Onesimus.

So here we are back in Romans and Paul wants Christians to live in peace and unity with others who are different for the love of Christ. Why are we to accept others and receive them into our hearts? Because when we were afar off Jesus came to us, when we were lying broken by the road of life he stopped to tend to us, when we were yet estranged sinners he died for us. If Jesus would do that for us, then we must do no less for others.

Why don't we accept someone and receive him or her into our heart? There are myriad reasons, I suppose, but perhaps the chief reason is that we put up walls to shield our hearts and to block acceptance. Sometimes it is only by the grace of God, literally assailing our shields and assaulting our defenses, that we have our hearts opened.

That happened to me long ago early in my ministry. Due to some unfortunate angry and violent encounters in high school, an unacknowledged prejudice developed in me toward Hispanic persons. No one knew it, for I kept it to myself, but it was there. And from that experience I learned that sometimes the experiences in early years can shut down our minds, or worse, close our hearts. It did mine.

Years later, I am working part time in an inner city church and one of my colleagues, Bill, falls ill. My assignment is to fill in for Bill by running the evening program in our church gym called "Open

Door to Life." Filling in for Bill was very uncomfortable for me. He had a charisma and an athleticism that I lacked and so I knew I could not do the job as well as he, and the program served almost exclusively Hispanic youths. (The "youths" were really young men in their late teens and early twenties.) Those seeds of prejudice planted in high school had grown into a distrust of Hispanics that was not warranted by any reality other than my small experience, and that first night the distrust was strong. Yet, I had a job to do and so I ran the program, interacted with the youth, kept the rules, and joined in on a few games. The night went well with a gym full of thirty young men playing hard and fair, challenging and sweating, laughing and joshing. When it came time to close I blew the whistle and shouted it was time to head home, and quickly the young men moved to put away the balls, equipment and games and head out the door. I stood at the top of the stairs by the exit to say goodbye, and as I stood there a strange thing happened. As the youth passed me to go out the door they all smiled at me, thanked me in English or Spanish, and they hit me. They punched me in the arm and shoulder, they slapped my back and playfully hit my chest and stomach as they went by, and with every hit the wall to my heart cracked and crumbled and fell.

My life gained a foundational truth that night. We will never be set free to truly live until the walls fall and the way to our hearts is opened and we can fully accept every other person as a precious creation of God and as a sister or brother loved by Christ.

Well, that is about racism, but there are other prejudices. Of course, there are. And so I must tell you about Suzy – which is not her name, but I must change it to protect her. It began a few years ago. I have a bad habit, especially around Christmas, of not opening my mail and it drives the woman I live with wild. The mail piles up and finally I open it. Well, there was an envelope that sat unopened on the counter for weeks, I suppose, and Christmas had come and was nearly to its Twelfth Day and still I had not opened it. One night as we prepared for bed Sally could no longer take it and announced, "I am opening this card." She opened it and said, "Why is a blond on the West Coast sending you a picture of herself?" I sleepily muttered, "I don't know. Maybe it's one of the ministers I helped." An

64

unconvinced voice said, "Well, she is very beautiful." I looked, and the woman was attractive but I did not have a clue as who she was. Sally started reading the note in the card and then said quietly, "Jeff, this is Jack.." Of course it isn't Jack my mind said. I knew Jack and that wasn't Jack, but, yet, still, there was something familiar in the face. Then I read the note.

It was Jack, who now was Suzy and in the card she was telling us that her life had changed and she wondered if she could come to see us. We were on the telephone that night – it was earlier out West – and we spoke to Suzy and told her to come.

Suzy did come to see us, and experienced some of the rush and confusion that is our lives. We talked in the living room and we talked over the dinner table and we talked on into the evening. We talked of memories, of friends, of our children, of faith and we talked of Suzy's new life. It was incredibly moving to hear someone I thought I knew – and I did know my friend well – reveal the deeper feelings and fears and dreams that had always been hers. She had always known she was a woman but she was born into a man's body and had done her best to be what family and society and culture expected. As a man she was a success, yet she carried hurt and sorrow within her that did not lessen but only grew with time's passage. Finally, while on a business trip and driving to Boston she decided that she could bear it no more and at high speed turned the car toward a bridge abutment. She believed the only way to end her pain was to take her life. What happened next is not clear but Suzy knows it was an angelic intervention and she next found herself sobbing and uninjured, holding onto the steering wheel of a wrecked car.

That highway to Boston was Suzy's Damascus Road experience. She knew she must stop living a lie and become the person God had made her to be. It was a long and lonely way she journeyed, enduring anger and rejection from many close to her, scorn and confusion from those who could accept her only as a man, yet wonderfully loved and accepted by her children. (Does that not say something wonderful about parents?) Suzy endured because she found strength from God to be who she was.

During that evening it came to me that my friend still sat across from me. Yes, the gender of my friend was different but her soul was the same. She was the same person, only less veiled and guarded and more real to herself and to me. I told her as we parted, "You are the same friend I've always admired and loved." She said, "Oh, thank you." And we hugged.

My sisters and brothers, we will never be set free to truly live until the walls fall and the way to our heart is opened and we can fully accept every other person as a precious creation of God and as a sister or brother loved by Christ.

Today the Church at large is beset with controversy about gays, lesbians and transgendered persons. The controversy over the newly elected and soon-to-be Bishop of New Hampshire is only the most visible part of the storms roiling the Church and the society it must speak to. There are no easy answers or simple solutions, but the Bible points to a way, and it is acceptance, receiving each other into our hearts and then in a relationship of loving acceptance working through all the other issues that occur when people with differences abide together. "Accept one another, then, just as Christ accepted you."

2005

Unity in Diversity
ROMANS 12:1-8

Rev. Paul Drake
Speed Memorial Church, Speed, Indiana

Paul exalts diversity in Romans 12, likening us to a body, each part with its ownrole to play.

"Just as each of us has one body with many members, and these members do not all have the same function, so in Christ we who are many form one body, and each member belongs to all the others." (Romans 12:4-5) Paul gives us a very good image of what the church is meant to be - one body with many members, each with his or her own function. Bill Cosby used to talk about how there was a war going on between the mind and the body. He said, "The mind is egotistical. It's the mind that says to the hand, when you have to get up in the middle of the night, 'Don't tum on that light! I know my way around here.' Meanwhile the toes are saying, 'Turn on the light, please! We're not goingthrough this again.'"

That's a humorous way of looking at this topic. But make no mistake about it;this is a very serious matter indeed. Our minds and bodies are amazing examples of unity. Not uniformity, mind you, but unity. Each part has its own function, but all are working together toward one goal: to build up and strengthen the body, the whole.

A number of years ago, I was on a car trip with a visitor from Brazil. Along the way we stopped at a gas station to fill up the tank and get some soda. Gerusa began reading the instructions on the top of her can of Coke. Showing how long ago this was, the new pull tabs on cans -you know, the kind that don't pull off but are attached, like we've all gotten used to now - had just come out. And there was printed instructions on the top of each can. They said, "1. Pull up

67

tab. 2. Push tab down. 3. Pull tab back." For some reason, we all found that hysterically funny, and began adding our own instructions to the list. "4. Open mouth. 5. Lift can. 6. Tilt can. 7. Pour soda. 8. Drink soda. 9.

Swallow. 10. Digest, and so on and on. I forget exactly how many steps we got out of that one simple act of drinking from a can. I'll bet you never realized taking a drink of Coke was such a complicated procedure.

But if you were making a flow chart to program a computer to drink soda from a can, you would have to break the process down into all those discrete steps. You couldn't assume the computer would do anything, no matter how small, without being told what to do and exactly how to do it. That's a clear demonstration of just how amazing our bodies really are. All the parts work together in unity, each performing its functions almost without even thinking about it.

But the parts are not all the same. If they were, we couldn't function at all. There are no two cells in my entire body (and at 6'2" and 235lbs., that covers a lot of territory) that are exactly alike. There are similar types of cells -   muscle, blood cells, nerves, bones, etc. But the body is not made up of just one of these types of cells, either. It would be a disaster if it were. As Paul points out when he deals with this topic another time, "If the whole body were an eye, how could it hear? And if it were only an ear, how

could it smell? As it is, however, God put every different part in the body just as he wanted it to be." (1 Corinthians 12:17-18)

I suspect that where I'm going next will leave some of you convinced I've gone off the deep end. Our Christian brothers and sisters in the Episcopal Church have been struggling with their decision to consecrate an openly homosexual bishop, the Rev. Gene Robinson of New Hampshire. His earlier selection by his Diocese was confirmed last summer by the House of Bishops by a vote of 62-45, not as close as some expected it to be. This action was taken despite threats and dire predictions of a split in the denomination as a result. While many local congregations and dioceses have undergone upheaval, the denomination here in the U.S. and the

Anglican Communion have stopped short of outright disunion, so far at least. We'll see what happens in the future.

I'll be honest and say outright that I applaud the Episcopal Church for having the courage to consecrate Bishop Robinson. If, as I believe and more and more Christians are beginning to believe, homosexuality is not a choice but the way a certain percentage of people are made to be, then Bishop Robinson and others like him could be some of those different parts of the body of Christ that God made "just as he wanted it to be", to quote that other Paul. That may be so even though a number of Christians reject the idea.

Our Sunday School class, as we have been studying Phil Yancey's book *What's So Amazing About Grace?*, struggled with the chapter he titled "Grace-Healed Eyes." There he writes about his long friendship with Mel White, an evangelical who used to work with the Christian Coalition and helped edit films for the Dobson group, Focus On the Family. Yancey talks about how shocked he was when, a few years ago, Mel came to him to say that he was gay and had been living a lie all those years. If you want to know all the details, you'll have to read the book (either Phil Yancey's or, better yet, Mel White's book, *Stranger at the Gate*).

The bottom line is that, although Phil couldn't agree with Mel's decision to leave his wife and come out of the closet, they remained friends. He quotes Mel White's mother, told by an interviewer that many Christians were calling her son an 'abomination': "Well, he may be an abomination, but he's still our pride and joy." Yancey sums up his comments by saying, "I came to see that Mel White's mother expressed how God views every one of us. In some ways we are all abominations to God - all have sinned and fall short of the glory of God - and yet somehow, against all reason, God loves us anyhow. Grace declares that we are still God's pride and joy."

Just remember, it hasn't been all that long ago that some Christians felt the same way and made the same arguments against the ordination of blacks or women. In fact, some Christian denominations are still struggling with accepting those different parts of the body as legitimate.

I think back to a time not so long ago at Speed Memorial Church, when MargaretStouffer was the first woman elected to the Board of Trustees. In the official church history, Veva Riggle Walker is mentioned as having served as deaconess some decades before, but that was during the war years of the 1940's, when many such things were done out of necessity. Electing a woman to the Church Council was a pretty controversial step to some members in 1978. Today, of course, nearly half of the Council members are women, and it's no longer shocking to see women serving the communion elements. Looking back from 25 years later, the idea that women should not be leaders inthe congregation seems downright silly.

My fervent hope is that one of these days we'll have advanced to the point where we welcome people of color in our pews and would be ready to accept a black or Hispanic Council member. And maybe somewhere down the line (hopefully when I'm ready to retire after 20-some glorious years in this pulpit) you all would be ready to accept a woman pastor, or a black or Hispanic pastor, or even, God forbid, a black or Hispanic woman pastor! And 25 years later, I hope the idea of *that* being something controversial would seem downright silly to new generations of church members.

I've been reading a book titled *The Passion Driven Congregation,* by Carver McGriff and Kent Millard. They have been pastors of St. Luke's United Methodist Church in Indianapolis for the past 38 years between them. During that time, the church grew from 300 members to over 5,000 members, with an average attendance in worship of 3,100. Listen to what Carver McGriff says he decided the church should be that led to such long, sustained growth. One of the first things a pastor must decide is the answer to the question, "What is a church?" That decision will determine the future for any congregation; I decided I would welcome everyone into my congregation. Old-time Methodists, of course. But so, too I'm on pretty solid ground so far, right? There's not too much disagreement with anything I've said up 'til now, I hope. But I just can't leave well enough alone. There's a reason for this, though. It's easy to talk about and achieve unity when we're all in agreement. But this sermon is about unity in diversity, just as I believe Paul meant when he said we are one body in Christ, but made up of many members with different gifts: homosexuals, divorced people, retired thieves, drug addicts, Presbyterians, struggling alcoholics, reforming prostitutes and Sunday morning golfers would be welcomed to my church. I encouraged my ordained colleagues to hold whatevertheological beliefs they chose so long as those beliefs did not produce prudish judgmentalism ... From the day I stepped into the pulpit of St. Luke's Church I insisted that anyone who walks through our door is welcome as part of our family. *(The Passion Driven Congregation, p. 22)*

I personally find that vision of the body of Christ a compelling and attractive one. To me, it's just a slight extension of Paul's stand in the first century. We constantly need to be reminded of the truth that the church is a hospital for sinners, not a haven for saints. Or, as J.B. Phillips insisted a generation or two ago, anytime you are tempted to exclude anyone, "Your God is too small." One author said about the Community Church Movement, "Our unity has not come from denying differences, has not come from ignoring the importance of differences. Our unity has developed from granting others the same freedom of personal faith and understanding we cherish for ourselves. The way to real unity lies in recognizing and accepting that uniformity is neither possible nor necessary in our changing world." (Sterling McHarg, in *Unity Without Uniformity*, p. 52)

Unity in diversity is tough, because it is human nature to make absolute judgments based on our highly individualized experiences of life. As Christians, though,we are called to rise above human nature. Unity in diversity is only possible when we learn to tolerate one another's differences, then to respect and value them, and finally to celebrate them.

One of the reasons I was drawn to the ICCC is that it remains the most integratedchurch organization in the United States. It does so in spite of the fact that the vast

majority of congregations in the ICCC are predominantly either black or white. Relatively few of our congregations are significantly racially mixed. But we all gain something when we get together and learn from each other. When my friend Herb Freitag, a white pastor of a largely white, suburban congregation, talks about his friendship with Dameau Stewart, a black pastor of an inner-city black congregation, I get goose bumps sometimes. The honesty and the love of that relationship, that is apparent in his voice 30 years after Dameau passed away, is a beautiful and transforming thing.

When Karen and I worshipped with my friend Matthew Stephens and his mostly black congregation at the Community Church of Cincinnati last summer, we experienced the joy of unity in diversity. When I see Marion Bascom and Bob Puckett (two older preachers now retired, one black and one white) hug each other and say to one another, with all sincerity, "I love you with the love of the Lord", I confess to being moved. To me, that's what Christianity should be and is all about.

I want to close by sharing a story from Tony Campolo's book *Let Me Tell You aStory*. Tomas Borge was a freedom fighter in the Nicaraguan revolution. He was captured and put in a dungeon. There he was chained to the wall, and in his helpless condition, was forced to watch as his captors dragged in his wife and gang raped her in front of him. Then they castrated him in an attempt to take away the last vestiges of manhood.

When the revolution had succeeded, Borge was released, and he paraded beforecheering crowds as one of the nation's heroes. But as he marched, he noticed in the crowd the face of one of his captors. It was one of the men who had raped his wife.

Borge broke ranks from the parade, ran over to where the man was standing, grabbed him by the shoulders, shook him and yelled, "Do you remember me? Do youremember me?"

The trembling and confused man could only answer in his fear, "Yes! Yes!"

The trembling man pretended he had never seen Borge before. But Borge persisted and screamed, "I will never forget your face! Never!" Then he asked, "Now do you understand what this revolution is all about?"

Borge responded, "No, you don't understand." Then he embraced the man and shouted, "I forgive you! I forgive you! That's what this revolution is all about!" *(Let Me Tell You a Story,)*

That is a reflection of the love Christ has for each of us in all our diversity.

Although we crucified him and put him through hell because of our sinfulness, he still embraces us and forgives us - each and every one of us. It is because of his great love and amazing grace that we are able to find unity in diversity. That's why I sing:

Your grace still amazes me.
Your love's still a mystery.
Each day, I fall on my knees
'Cause your grace still amazes me. (Shawn Craig and Connie Harrington)

Amen.

2006

WORLD WIDE COMMUNION SUNDAY
How Big is your Table?

Keith R. Haverkamp
Norris Religious Fellowship, Norris, TN

The people of the church community were building a new church. It was a fine building, its pinnacle reaching to God. The architect had done a fine job of designing the structure, the board and the people had approved the design with little dissent, and what differences there were, were quickly forgotten or put aside for the common good.

There was excitement in the air as the foundation was laid and the first beams were put in place. Work days were festive events and the men, the woman and the children each in their own way contributed to the building, using their God given gifts and abilities to create the new building in which to worship and praise God.

There were many details to be attended to: The framing of the windows, the pews (dark or light), the color of the carpet, windows (clear or stained glass) the woodwork that housed the candles, the lectern and pulpit, the choir loft, and the communion table. There were a number of skilled craftsmen in the fellowship, among them skilled carpenters and woodworkers.

One of the carpenters was chosen to make the communion table and when he got ready to make the table he carefully selected the finest woods and began to sketch out a design that he thought would be fitting for the building as well as a tribute to the remembrance of Christ. He went to the project superintendent and asked how big the table should be. "How big should the communion table be? He asked.

The building superintendent said, "Well, I guess I'm not really sure, let's go and ask the architect." So they did. They said, "How big should the communion table be?"

He replied "I'm not really sure, it might be not only a question of the size in the building but the theology of the church." So they went to the Board, told them the problem and asked how big the communion table should be. The Board discussed it for a week and then decided to ask the minister. "Pastor," they said, "We have a problem and we know that you have had vast and extensive training in these matters. Tell, us how big should the communion table be?" The minister was gratified in the trust placed in him and took the matter very seriously. He thought about it for a week consulted some other churches and met with some of the ministers at the local coffee shop to discuss their understanding of the communion table; all without a satisfactory answer. He told the Board they should appoint a committee to discuss the matter. It was proving to be a much bigger issue than he would have imagined. It took the Board another week to form a committee and they met a week later and talked about it for two weeks, did a poll of the congregation, did some internet research, and then they decided to make some church visits. They made a chart on Excel, took their tape measures and went to a number of churches and composed an impressive list of details, height, width, depth, length, types of wood, inscriptions and methods of constructions. But they were still stymied. "How big should the communion table be," and they still had no good answer to what was appearing to be a very important question.

The church had a Sunday school program that encouraged exploration and diversity in the midst of its biblical studies. Not only did they research and study the Bible stories and meaning in detail, but they also took time to study other cultures and traditions. For instance, they studied the way in which other cultures celebrated Christmas. And they studied other religions, such as Buddhism, Hinduism, Native American spirituality and Islam. The church felt it important that they know something about other faiths and peoples. They also taught respect for these faith traditions while at the same time upholding the value meaning and truths of their own faith.

Well, World Wide Communion Sunday was coming and the Sunday school classes were studying the sacrament so as to better understand it. The teachers had taught that that the communion table held the sacraments for the worshippers. They had also discussed how communion was for the entire world, everyone could come, and celebrate the gifts of communion. They also talked about World Wide Communion Sunday and how all across the earth, all Christians everywhere celebrated the sacrament on this day.

As part of the learning process, one of the classes was making drawings of the sacrament of communion and the process of partaking. The pictures showed the communion table, bread and juice, candles and the people eating and praying. They were wonderful pictures. One little child took a very long time to complete the drawing but when it was finally finished the child proudly presented it to all of the teachers. The drawing was quite large and quite different from the rest of the drawings. It depicted a communion table that was not contained within the church but stretched out from the center of the church through the church walls and wrapped around the entire earth, literally embracing the earth like a belt. Not only did the communion table enfold the entire world, but seated at the table were people of all colors and sizes and types sharing in the communion meal. In fact, not only were there Christians, but upon being asked, the child identified people from India who he said were Hindus and Buddhists, and people from Japan who studied Confucius and people from the middle east who were Moslems, and Native Americans, and people from all over the earth of every faith color and belief. The teacher asked about the drawing and the child said, "Well, you said that communion was God's gift for everyone and that whole world was invited." "Yes, I did say that," said the teacher. "You said, we Christians were hospitable people, welcoming and loving," "Yes, I did say that," said the teacher.

"So I made the table big enough for the whole world and for everyone, no matter what."

The teachers of course, knew that the church was wrestling with the question, "How big should the communion table be?" so they took the drawing and the child to the communion table committee and the drawing was shown and the child explained the communion table to the committee, who explained it to the Board, who explained it to the pastor, who explained it to the building superintendent, who explained it to the carpenter who explained it to the architect, and so began a new process of understanding in the church about its role in the world and the role of the sacrament of communion in the world.

Decisions were made, as a new understanding fell into place and the whole process instead of being labored and technically difficult and worrisome became a joy. It was as if God was making the decisions and had blessed the event. This is what the church decided to do, or maybe, God decided. A stained glass artist who was a member of the church was commissioned to make a large stained glass window based upon the child's drawing and it became the center piece of the sanctuary. The communion table itself was not a table at all but a thick piece of clear Plexiglas that hung from the ceiling on thick invisible line in front of the stained glass window. When the bread and the cup of juice were set on this table, they seemed suspended in mid air and appeared to be sitting on the table of stained glass that stretched around the earth. On the first Sunday when all was in place, it was very still and solemn in the church as the congregation absorbed the meaning of God's universal love spread before them. The title of the sermon was, "How big is your table?" The scripture was read by the teacher, "Beloved let us love one another because love is from God, and everyone who loves is born of God, and knows God. Beloved, since God loved us so much we also ought to love one another. No one has ever seen God; if we love one another, God lives in us, and his love is perfected in us…we are the dwelling place of God."

2007

TO BE A MAN

Bob Puckett 2007
Tellico Village Community Church
Loudon, TN.

Today is a very special day, it is the day we honor fathers.

It takes real courage to stand up and be counted for what is right. But that is exactly what good fathers do.

I want to tell you a true story about a man named Rufus Jones. He was a Quaker mystic who learned very early in life to stand up for what is right.

One morning when Rufus was still quite young, his widowed mother went into town to shop, leaving young Rufus to do some chores which very much needed doing.

The boy fully intended to obey his mother, but the temptation to go fishing instead was too strong.

He was sure that he was going to be severely punished when his mother returned.

Instead, his mother, her voice heavy with sad disappointment, called him to her bedroom. Instead of punishing him, she had him get down on his knees and she knelt beside him. Then with an arm around his shoulder and tears in her eyes, she prayed, "Lord, make a man out of him."

Dr. Jones said that this incident did more to guide his life in a positive direction than any physical punishment could ever have done.

The trouble these days seems to be that there is a great deal of confusion about what it takes to make a man out of anyone.

Many years ago Dr. Charles Trentham and I attended the College of Ministers at Morehouse College at the Martin Luther King Chapel in Atlanta. We were the only white persons to register. Charles said that we were winners because we were the best looking white people present.

Dr. Dexter Wise, who calls himself "The Rappin' Reverend" was one of the speakers. I can't do it the way he did, but here is part of what he said:

Every little boy wants to be a man,
shave every day as soon as he can,
drive a fast car,
make the women go wild,
turn all their heads as he bops down the aisle.
The problem is to know what kind of man you ought to be,
you don't get much help from just watching TV,
If you want to be a man,
Let me tell you. It's not easy but you can.
Being a man means responsibility,
A father, a husband, and supporting a family.
Want to be a man?
It's not easy but you can.

And of course, the best way to learn what it means to be a real man is to learn from our Heavenly Father.

All of us fathers need someone to pray that same prayer that Rufus Jones' mother prayed for him "Lord, make a man out of him."

TO BE A MAN IN THE BEST SENSE IS TO LEARN WHAT REAL MANHOOD IS FROM OUR HEAVENLY FATHER!

PRAYER: WE THANK YOU, O GOD, FOR REAL MEN WHO LEARN ABOUT WHAT KIND OF MEN THEY SHOULD BE FROM YOU. WE THANK YOU FOR THE GOOD INFLUENCE THAT FATHERS HAVE UPON THEIR SONS AND DAUGHTERS

2008

One Church
JOHN 17:20-26

William F. Schnell
Senior Minister of The Church in Aurora
Delivered May 20, 2007

When people tell us that they are Catholic, we have a pretty good idea what that means. We may not know the finer details of Roman Catholic theology, but we have a general idea about what Catholics believe. If somebody is a Southern Baptist, we have a pretty good idea as to what that is all about. The same goes for Methodists, Presbyterians, Lutherans and Episcopalians. We know the Amish do not use electricity, they wear distinctive clothing, and they ride in buggies.

But not many people know what is distinctive about Community Churches because we are not a very big fellowship of churches and are therefore not too well known. Perhaps someone has inquired as to your church membership. When you told them you belonged to a community church, did they get a quizzical look on their face and ask, "What are Community Churches like? What do they believe?" Have you ever felt at a loss for words to describe how we might be like other churches and how we might be distinctive?

In the New Testament we read: "Always be prepared to give an answer to everyone who asks you to give the reason for the hope that you have." (I Peter 3:15). Allow me to help you be prepared to give an answer the next time someone asks you about the family of faith to which you belong. The key to that answer is in the word "Community." You will notice that on the front of our bulletin, under "The Church in Aurora," we read in parenthesis (Community). On the back of our bulletin is a statement that explains what that means: "A member church of the International Council of Community Churches."

Okay that still begs the question, "What are Community Churches?" A further statement defines the International Council of Community Churches, to wit: "A fellowship of ecumenically minded, freedom-loving churches cooperating in fulfilling the mission of the Church in the World." One of the definitions for ecumenical in the dictionary is: "Concerned with establishing or promoting unity among churches or religions."

The word "community" pretty much sums up what is distinctive about Community Churches. The distinctive thing about Community Churches is that they emphasize the *common unity* of all believers. What do we all have in common? We are all God's children, for starters. There is one God and Father of us all; and, like most parents, it drives God nuts when his children fuss and fight with one another. So when people ask you what Community Churches are all about, just say they are big on promoting Christian Unity. Otherwise they are pretty much like other mainline Protestant Churches such as Methodists, Presbyterians, Lutherans and so forth.

The biggest and broadest ecumenical organization in America is the National Council of Churches. Guess who the current President is. Our own Michael Livingston, the Executive Director of the International Council of Community Churches. Guess who is a voting delegate to the annual General Board meeting of the same organization? Me! I get to schmooze with all sorts of big wigs because Community Churches are involved on the ecumenical scene all out of proportion to our diminutive size.

Last week we announced the untimely passing of Rev. Jeff Newhall, the immediate past Executive Director of the International Council of Community Churches. He was also a leader in a movement called "Churches Uniting in Christ" and will soon be recognized in the national press as a great ecumenist—a great proponent of Christian Unity in particular and religious unity in general. I can hardly think of a more needful message in this age of religiously fueled hatred.

Our text assigned for this morning by the Revised Common Lectionary is the most often quoted text in the Community Church Movement. That is because it provides the clearest biblical foundation for Christian Unity. It is not the only text to provide such a foundation, to be sure. But it is the preeminent text used in our literature and alluded to time and again in Community Church circles. Although the message has been preached upon many times by Community Church ministers, it has not been "preached out."

The title of our message for today is "One Church." That happens to be the actual name of a church in Arizona pastored by a gentleman friend of Hannah Horak. I like the name of that church. It may not be a member church of the International Council of Community Churches, but it has a name any community church could be proud of: "One Church." One church among many. One body of Christ made up of many member/parts. One in spirit. One for all and all for one. I like it. That, we will see, is the kind of church for which Christ prayed.

Our text is part of a larger prayer that Jesus is offering just prior to his arrest and trial and crucifixion. In fact, our text is comprised of the very last words of Jesus before his arrest occurred. I would say that this parting prayerful message is climactic to say the least. First Jesus prays for himself, and then he prays for his disciples. In our text Jesus continues: "My prayer is not for them alone. I pray also for those who will believe in me through their message." (Verse 20). That would include you and me and all who have come to believe through the Gospel witness.

And for what does Jesus pray? "That all of them may be one, Father, just as you are in me and I am in you." (Verse 21). Jesus prays that believers will be one with each other just like he and the Father are one. How are he and the Father one? Paul writes: "The Son is the radiance of God's glory and the exact representation of his being." (Hebrews 1:3). And again, "He is the image of the invisible God." (Colossians 1:15) Like father, like son. To know one is to know the other. If we want to see what God is like in human form, look at Jesus. In this way the Father and Son are one.

Just as Jesus is a reflection of God, so the Church is a reflection of Jesus. Indeed, the Church is the body of Christ on earth—his continuing physical presence on earth and his continuing ministry on earth. Jesus naturally wants the Church to be a good reflection on him and not a bad one, just as we want our children to be a good reflection on us. If our children are contentious, abrasive and rude, that is not a very good reflection on us as parents. In the same way, if believers who take the name of Jesus are contentious, abrasive and rude, that is not a very good reflection on Jesus.

Mahatma Gandhi is regarded as the father of the Indian nation. His writings have influenced great religious leaders such as Martin Luther King Jr. When Gandhi was young, he was disheartened by his country's caste system that was supported by his Hindu faith tradition. While visiting South Africa he became impressed with Christianity as a religious alternative that promised hope for overcoming such unfair and hurtful social barriers.

One Sunday, hoping to approach the minister about receiving instruction in the Christian faith, he went to attend services at a Christian church. But the ushers at the service refused him a seat because of his dark skin. They asked him, "Why don't you visit the colored peoples' church?" Gandhi never became a Christian. "If Christians also have differences, I might as well remain a Hindu," he explained. The divisiveness of that Christian Church in South Africa was a bad reflection on Jesus Christ.

This is why Jesus prays, "that all of them may be one, Father, just as you are in me and I am in you. May they also be in us so that the world may believe that you have sent me." (Verse 21). Who is going to believe that Jesus has anything to do with God if the people who bear his name, and the church that bears his name, behave in such hurtful and hateful ways? Who wants to attend a church where people are fussing and fighting all the time? Who has time for that kind of stress? There is enough stress like that in the world without having to go to church to find more.

When there is painful division in the Church, whether we are talking about divisions in the local church or divisions among the denominations that make up "the larger church," there is something wrong with that picture. If we are all God's children and God loves us with a perfect love, then you know he wants us to love one another. Not to love God's other children is tantamount to saying, "God does not love you, and neither do I." But this is not the message Jesus is trying to get across. Again he prays, "May they be brought to

83

complete unity to let the world know that you sent me and have loved them even as you have loved me." (Verse 23).

This prayerful plea is Jesus parting message just before his arrest and crucifixion. It is his dying wish for those who will follow after him. Community Churches believe in honoring Jesus' final wish. Community Churches believe in One Church–not one institutional church, but many institutional churches that are one in spirit. Two of our favorite slogans are "Unity Without Uniformity," and, "Diversity Without Divisiveness." We do not always achieve it, but it is the ideal toward which we strive, and it explains a lot about how we operate.

So when Father Joe Witmer of Our Lady of Perpetual Help Church in Aurora celebrated the fortieth anniversary of his ordination yesterday, Nancy and I were at the dinner reception representing The Church in Aurora. As an amazing coincidence, Father Joe's commitment to ecumenism (Christian unity) is emphasized in his commemorative bulletin together with the words of our text for this morning: "that all may be one, as the Father and I are one."

When the Aurora United Methodist Church celebrates its fiftieth anniversary today, their members will find a page in their commemorative booklet provided by The Church in Aurora that will read: "The congregation, leadership and staff of The Church in Aurora celebrates with The Aurora United Methodist Church on the occasion of 50 years of faithful service to our community and world. May the next 50 years and beyond find us laboring side-by-side in the fields of the Lord that have been our common portion."

In these and many other ways we promote unity in the community— the local community, the church community and the world community. When folks ask you what the Community Church is about just tell them that the term "Community" says it all—*common unity*. We seek to embody the Christian unity for which our Lord prayed. Otherwise, we are like any other family of faith. And when people ask you about our funny name, just tell them that The Church in Aurora is not the only church in Aurora. It is one church among many. It is one in spirit with all believers, regardless of denominational affiliation. And just like "The Larger Church," it is one body of believers made up of many different parts because, as the hymn says, "Our God has made us one."

2009

OBAMA, THE ICCC AND ME
SCRIPTURE: GALATIANS 3:23-29

Hary Foockle
Antioch Community Church
Kansas City, Missouri

SERMON THE WEEK AFTER THE HISTORIC ELECTION OF BARACK OBAMA

"THIS IS NOT ABOUT CLASS NOR COLOR, RACE OR CREED/ MAKE NO MISTAKE, IT'S THE CHANGES, WHAT ALL THE PEOPLE THEM NEED."

Those are some of the words of Cocoa Tea (a Reggae singer from Jamaica) before the election of Barack Obama.
If he is correct...then what are the changes we need? How does it relate to the ICCC? Me? You?
Let us go directly to the obvious...this was indeed a historic election with the first African American elected to the highest office in the land and it will make him one of the most powerful persons in the world. This happens just some 143 short years after the ending of the Civil War in America. This happens when we still struggle with racial and economic injustice.
So we have bridged the gap. Race relations in America have stabilized. Prejudice and bias on the streets, in our schools and in the workplace has ended and it is over! Really?
Someone forgot to tell the folks in Missouri City, Missouri it was over. Just a few weeks ago (after Barack Obama defeated Hillary Clinton in the primary) close to Kansas City in a small Missouri town which houses the smallest school district in the state the following took place.

It was a Tuesday evening, just before midnight, an Interracial husband and wife and their two children were awakened to a loud voice in their front yard at Missouri City. The voice said, "N.......... (and used the word which I refuse to say) lover. I'm going to kill the N.......lover, your wife, your children." The man beat upon their door and shouted other obscene threats.

That man (their neighbor) is now in jail awaiting action on a hate crime charge. A group of us held a rally of support in Missouri City for the family who were the victims. We are awaiting the outcome of the charges. In the meantime we prayed and gave support to the family. We also prayed for the man charged who was a victim of his own prejudice and hatred.

Prejudice and bias on the streets, in our schools and in the workplace has ended and it is over! Really?

The day after the election members of Antioch Church (snowbirds living in Yuma, Arizona for the winter) greeted their neighbor who was just arriving for the winter from Branson, Missouri. Some pleasantries about the trip were exchanged and he said to our member Jeri, "Well how does it feel to have a N.......(and he used the word which I still refuse to say) elected as President of the United States?"

Bless her heart she responded much calmer than I would have. After she told him about her grandson who is black and serving in Iraq and who speaks 4 different languages and serves as an interpreter for our government...after that she wished him a good day...went back into their home and prayed for this man who was a victim of his own prejudice and hatred as much as the man from Missouri City.

Prejudice and bias on the streets, in our schools and in the workplace has ended and it is over! Really? No, it is not over! It has come a long way, but it is not over.

The 3rd chapter of Galatians and verse 28 reads "There is neither Jew nor Greek, there is neither bond nor free, there is neither male nor female, for we are all one in Christ Jesus."Those words need to be the focus of our efforts as individuals and as a community of faith. If we are faithful to God's call and share this Good News with others around us then our lives and the lives of our community will be better. Perfect? No, but better.

I remember in Seminary the words of John Wesley (Founder of what is the Methodist movement) of how we are to "strive toward perfection." Our truth is found in the striving. If we ever quit striving then prejudice, bias, hatred, and economic injustice will win.

Will we succeed in bringing everyone to "strive toward perfection?" No, but to forgo the effort to try is to allow prejudice to win.

One of the reasons I love the ministry of the International Council of Churches is because it is a "striving" movement. From its inception it has sought to build bridges instead of walls. It has sought to work in harmony across racial and gender barriers.

We are a ground breaking movement in American church history, but our work is not finished. Fields still need to be plowed. Seeds still need to be planted. Our world yearns for a harvest of love and acceptance. We have been blessed by God because those pioneers ahead of us stepped out in faith that the Gospel was right. We are all equal in the sight of God. To stop the work and say now that we have elected an African American president we have arrived and can rest is to allow the hatred that still lurks in the corners to come out because our guard will be down. It would allow the man to stand in the yard and yell the slurs at his neighbors or worse…No, No, No we cannot allow it…not if we are committed to Galatians 3.

Finally, a personal plea to continue to live as the ICCC has led us and Cocoa Tea has said…"make no mistake it's the changes, what all the people them need." The change of minds and hearts to truly rejoice at the election because in America and as the Gospel says "we are all one…"

I grew up in West Texas a place and time where we were divided by colored waiting rooms and white waiting rooms at the bus stops. Where the drinking fountain for coloreds was around the back. Where the man at the Dairy Queen would only serve the coloreds at the back door and then only if he felt like it.

It was a town divided into three sections. They called them…Mexican town, Queen City and the Whites in the middle. Not only did the divisions happen in the bus stations, the Dairy Queens and city boundaries, but worse yet is they separated us as people from one

88

another because of skin color. If you were not white then you were inferior. I grew up believing that. My daddy used to tell me when you leave high school and go on to college and play football you may have to play against "those people." He told me that (and he would use the N.....word which I refuse to say) they have weak shin bones so if you get in the game hit them in the shins and it will be over for them. Then I got in my first football game and was hit in the shin (ouch and double ouch) it hurt so bad and I thought later after the pain was over, wait a minute something is not right. I mean I was white not black...if I hurt maybe we all hurt the same. Hold on here...could it mean that other than the color of the outside of our bodies we were really the same? The answer for me came quite clear years later, when in the military, an African American man from Chicago saved my life. I would discover our hearts were the same. My heart began to change. I realized I loved my Daddy, but my Daddy was wrong. I vowed to live a life of change and try to be an example for others. I would yearn for and work for Galatians 3 to become everyone's goal in life. I wanted my children to say, "I love my Daddy and my Daddy was right." I would become involved in The Southern Christian Leadership Conference led by Dr. Martin Luther King, Jr. Years later (which brings us to today) I would cross paths with this movement called the ICCC and discover a whole host of others in church who strive for and live in acceptance of others. I am at home.

The icing on the cake is the historic election of Barack Obama, just a few short years after the Civil War in America when a Free Black Man by the name of Martin called us to freedom and gave his life doing so...and an African by the name of Nelson suffered through fall of Apartheid. I cannot imagine what joy African Americans must feel at this moment...how much greater than my joy as someone who has never suffered the kind of injustice they have, but who has been "striving" all these years to bring change. I have found Jesus...I have seen Galatians working...I became a part of the ICCC...YES I AM HOME!!! I invite you to come home with me!!!

Skeletons in the Closet
RUTH 3:1-5; 4:13-17

Rev. Martin C. Singley III

We all love to hear about skeletons in the closet–of other people!

Strom Thurmond, radical segregationist, after his death at age 100, it comes out that he had fathered a secret child, a daughter, conceived out of a relationship with a *black* servant-girl when he was twenty-two and she was fifteen. Oh my, skeletons in the closet!

There is actually a web page called "The Skeleton Closet" where you can get all the dirt on all of the Presidential candidates of any given year; and, let me tell you, there're a lot of bones in those closets!

Maybe there are skeletons in *your* closet, too – secrets, mistakes, embarrassing family members. Skeletons in the closet!

George Bernard Shaw once said, "If you can't get rid of the skeleton in your closet, you'd best teach it to dance" – which brings us to the Old Testament book of Ruth!

Everybody loves the story of Ruth. It begins with a Jewish family leaving their hometown of Bethlehem because a terrible famine has swept through the land. Elimelech and his wife Naomi take their two sons and go down to Moab to start a new life. While there, the boys meet two beautiful Moabite women, Orpah and Ruth. They are smitten! They fall in love. They get married, and life is good until one of those tragic turnarounds comes along. The swine flu or some other terrible epidemic sweeps through the countryside and the three men die. The three women are left as widows–Naomi, Orpah, and Ruth. Knowing that the only place she can survive is back home among her kinfolk, Naomi decides to go home to Bethlehem. She blesses Orpah and Ruth, telling them to go back to their own families and get on with their lives. Orpah leaves, but Ruth will not go. She speaks to her mother-in-law Naomi those famous words that are often read in wedding ceremonies today: "Entreat me not to leave you, or to turn back from following you. For whither you go, I will go, where you stay, I will stay; your people will be my people, and your God, my God. Where you die, I will die, and there will I be buried" (Ruth 1:16-17).

Lovely words, beautiful sentiments of commitment, and if there are any folks here today who haven't heard the story, these are very special words to Bob and Jane Puckett. They were living over in Norris, Tennessee, serving the Community church there after having lived for quite a few years in Buffalo, New York. One day, Bob received a letter from a search committee in Buffalo asking if he'd be interested in returning to that area to serve their church. Bob called Jane on the phone and read the letter. "What do you think?" Bob asked. Jane said, "Well, Robert, I've always been like Ruth: "whither thou goest, I will go"; but I ain't gonna whither back to Buffalo!"

Back to the Bible: The story of Ruth is cherished because it is a story of loving devotion between Ruth and her mother-in-law. It is a touching story about the power of love when love is steadfast and true. And it assures us that love brings us good things sooner or later. And that's a good teaching, especially when we are facing moments when it would be easier not to love. But as good a teaching as that is, it's not really what the story of Ruth is about. Ruth is about a skeleton in a closet.

The book of Ruth is a type of biblical writing that is called "protest literature." It is a kind of writing that is included in the Bible to counteract or counterbalance other writings in the Bible. In this case, the book of Ruth is protesting against a passage in Deuteronomy 23 that says, "No Ammonite or Moabite or any of his descendants may enter the assembly of the Lord even down to the tenth generation" meaning "forever!" No Moabites allowed!

In other times and places, such a law might say: "No Irish Need Apply," "Blacks Sit In Back," "God Hates Gays," "The Final Solution."

Do you hear what this passage is saying? Some people are worthy of being excluded. And the reason Moabites are not allowed? When the Israelites were making their way from Egypt to the Promised Land, they passed through the land of Moab, and the Moabites wouldn't help them. The Israelites were non-citizen aliens who wanted food and shelter and jobs, and the Moabites were frightened that this huge stream of migrants would consume their land. In Numbers 22:4, the Moabites express their fear, "This horde is going to lick up everything around us, like an ox licks up the grass of the ground." Get the picture?

They sound a lot like people today who fear that undocumented workers from Mexico and other places will consume all of our hard-earned resources. So we can understand how the Moabites must have felt. So they did not help the Israelites. And the Israelites never forgot. And once settled in their own land, they made a law that said, "No Moabites allowed up to the tenth generation," meaning "forever!" And they called it the law of God.

That's human nature, isn't it? We take our hurts, our injuries, our self-serving values, our limited perspective on life, our prejudices, our fears, our likes and dislikes, our human opinions, even our personal tastes; and we elevate them to the level of divine law!

"God helps those who help themselves!" That's not found anywhere in the Bible, you know, but people would swear that it is a law of God. "Clapping in church is inappropriate!" That contradicts what the Psalms tell us to do when we worship, but people would have us think it's a sin to clap, or laugh in church, let alone sit in someone else's pew!

Do you hear what I'm saying? We human beings try to impose our ways and thoughts upon each other by putting our own words into God's mouth! That's why we love to pull out a verse from here and a verse from there in the Bible to prove the point we want to make. And any point you want to make *can* be proof-texted that way! *Moabites not allowed*!

Or you can substitute the name of some other person or group of your choice to be excluded. Religious people are all-the-time-finding-excuses for making someone else not welcome at the table of the Lord. But then along comes a story like the story of Ruth, the story of a skeleton in someone's closet!

How wonderful God is not to let sinful, human ideas even those memorialized in the scriptures go unchallenged. So God inspires some unknown author to write a story that protests against that verse in Deuteronomy 23. He or she pens a tale about a Moabite woman named Ruth. Unlike the Jewish stereotype of people from Moab that portrays them as uncaring, unhelpful, unloving folks, Ruth is just the opposite. She is the epitome of love! She does not reject Naomi the Jew. Ruth does not refuse her the help she needs. No, Ruth binds herself to Naomi. "Entreat me not to leave you, or to turn back from following you, for where you go I will go, where you lodge, I will lodge; your people shall be my people, and your God, my God. Where you die, I shall die, and there shall I be buried." Ruth gives a beautiful, loving, human face to the Moabite people. The stereotype is shattered. The conventional wisdom is shown to not be wisdom at all.

And the best part of the story is that Ruth the Moabite marries a Jewish man named Boaz. They have a son named Obed. Obed has a son named Jesse, and Jesse has a son named David, who became the greatest king of Israel!

Oh, David had a skeleton in his closet! His great-grandmother was a dirty rotten Moabite! And of course, you know that makes Ruth the great, great, great, great – and so on – grandmother of Jesus, the descendant of David! Skeletons in the closet!

So what can we learn from the story of Ruth, our spiritual skeleton in the closet? Well, first of all, from a very personal point of view, don't let other people define who you are and how you must live. Had Ruth given in to the voices of those who saw her as "one of those people," David would not have become king, and Jesus would not have been born! Instead, Ruth claimed God's definition of herself: "your people shall be my people, and your God, my God."

Only God has the right to say who you really are. Others may see you for some flaw in your heritage, some indiscretion in your past, some failure in your relationships, some part of your life that doesn't meet others' expectations, some sin or sins you've committed; and they will beat those things over your head until you give in to the notion that you are a nameless nobody defined by those flaws, a skeleton in someone's closet.

But God sees us differently. God sees you as his beloved child, as one who has the potential to become all that God created you to be, as a person of worth and tremendous value – a person with a future! And it is only when you take up God's definition of you instead of everybody else's that you can discover the full measure of the person God created you to be!

Ruth refused to be regarded as just another Moabite. She was a child of God, capable of great goodness and love! And so are you!

A second thing we can learn from Ruth is that none of us has the right to look down our noses at anybody else. There are skeletons enough to go around if that's how we want to measure other people, and to be measured *by* other people. Sandy has done a lot of work on our families' genealogies. Don't even ask! There are more rascals, unwed parents, divorces, suicides, drunks, and failures than we can count! And then there's us! And we've got our own baggage!

Of all the things Jesus taught us not to do, judging others is at the top. Why? Because God will hold you to the same standard of judgment that you impose on others. The judgment you give is the judgment you're going to get. And why is judging others such a serious sin? Because it destroys people and even nations.

So instead of looking *down* at others, look *up* to them! See them as people God created – people who, just like you, are doing their best to raise families, to find happiness, to make their way through this very challenging world.

And finally, learn from the story of Ruth that the community is strengthened when we welcome strangers and take care of people others exclude. That's one of the reasons I so strongly believe in this Community Church concept that refuses to close in on itself and to care exclusively for its own needs without regard to others, but chooses to open its arms and doors to all who would come.

I believe in a church that welcomes Moabites! So go this week, and claim your identity as a beautiful child of God! Live out that beauty by looking up to and loving others! And work hard to help us be the kind of church that understands that even skeletons in the closet have names like Ruth. Thanks be to God!

2011

Devoted to Community

ACTS 2:42.

Week of prayer for Christian Unity.

Fran Salone-Pelletier
Lead Chaplain at Brunswick Community Hospital,
Author of Awakening to God: The Sunday Readings in Our Lives(a trilogy of Scriptural meditations).

Had I known what the readings, especially the Gospel, were for this event, I think I'd have been silent when the question arose: "Who is going to preach this year?" It is challenging enough to be presented with the need for Christian unity in the midst of the wondrous diversity we all maintain. But to add to that challenge a call and commission to stretch ourselves toward an ideal community is to raise the bar. To deepen it by reminding ourselves that we really have no other choice but to seek unity no matter how differently we express our Christianity goes beyond being a challenging mission. It is the lifestyle, the life breath of Christianity. We avoid it, deny it, or ignore it at our peril.

Those are hard and harsh words. I am reluctant to say them aloud. I don't even want to whisper them to myself. The words bring me face to face with a question that does more than simply prick my conscience. It confronts my consciousness of Christianity, of discipleship and evangelization. The question that I hear emerging from the Scriptures is, "Can I call myself a Christian, can we call ourselves Christians, and still remain unreconciled with each other? From that question other concerns are evoked. What do we need to do in order to attain unity? Must we be clones of each other? Can I maintain my present denominational affiliation while acknowledging the truth of another denomination?

When we look at the three readings selected for this worship service, the answer becomes clear. It's not an easy road to follow. It

96

is not a reality that will necessarily change overnight. After all, it has taken us years to develop our love for our own way of doing things, our own theologies, our own liturgies, our own rules and regulations. We have formed and re-formed the church since its earliest days. The apostles had differences of opinion. They had to expand their understanding of what it meant to follow the Way of Christ. Their trust in the letter of the law was shaken when they were faced with the problem of accepting uncircumcised Gentiles as members of the church.

Christians have argued and discussed what it means to follow Jesus from apostolic days to the present time. We looked for specific answers in Scripture and are continuing to do so yet we find directives that only specify, "Come, and see. Come, follow me." Jesus apparently wasn't and isn't interested in choosing one denomination over another. He just wants us to come and see where he is. He wants us to follow him. There were no Methodist, Episcopal, Lutheran,Presbyterian, Baptist, Roman Catholic, Non-denominational churches then. Jesus was a Jew. So, what are we to do? Isaiah (58:6ff) gives us both a direction in which to go and directives to follow. Here is our biblical GPS. How can we be one? The first thing is to fast from personal biases, prejudices and/or theologies that exclude understandings of God that differ from ours. Isaiah tells us to do the kind of fasting that God desires. We are to fast from holding others hostage. Release them from the unjust bonds we have used to tie them into knots. Set free all those we have oppressed with our self-righteousness, our narrow understanding of divinity, our judgments and severe criticism. Free them from the guilt and shame we have heaped upon them because they do not meet our standards of spiritual excellence.

Share our bread with the hungry, shelter the homeless, and clothe the naked. Do not turn our backs on anyone.

I suspect that the Isaiah commands go deeper than physical freeing and feeding. I suspect we are being called to compassionate living. I suspect we are being challenged to recognize our own needs, our own hunger for God-the fullness of our being, our own thirst for a spiritual life, our own imprisonment.

When we begin to live as Isaiah commands, something wondrous happens we change. That's right, we change! Our concentration is no longer on making others become like us. We begin to notice that we are being transformed individually and communally. We are transformed into the people of God. The divine light that we had kept hidden or obscured within the confines of our individual denominations breaks forth. The wounds of division within us and outside of us are healed. Light rises from our darkness. Gloom becomes like midday. We clearly hear God's promise, "Here, I am." Truly, God is in our midst.

God is in our midst when we stay together, holding all things in common. God is in our midst while we are sharing the bread of our existence, the meat of our belief systems. God is in our midst as we sell our property. God is in our midst as we dispose of our possessions-the ideas we thought were ours alone, the faith we narrowed into an exclusive ownership. God would have to be in our midst because we could never achieve this relinquishing of cherished goods on our own.

It has been said that everybody wants unity. All of us desire it from the bottom of our hearts. We are made for unity because we are made for happiness. We get knots in our stomachs when we are in family situations or other groups where one person is not speaking to another. We get a sinking feeling when we find ourselves in the middle of an unpleasant encounter where two people are at each others' throats in argumentation. We want it to go away. We want everything and everyone to get along.

Perhaps, we think the solution is to have unity centered in our viewpoint. My father used to proclaim on a rather frequent basis, "If you people would listen to me and do what I want, everything would be fine." That translated into a submission that was more akin to enslavement than it was to freedom. We were not free to speak our minds, to offer our suggestions and ideas. We were free only to do what Daddy said.

God is not that kind of Daddy. God's parenting style is one of openness, of listening, of loving all of us unconditionally and promising to be with us no matter what we are or what we do. God's parenting style must be ours if we are to be God's people. We are to be people who are *forgiving.* That's our aim: to give and to receive. Our goal is not *forgetting.* Our mission is not to get others to come to our church, our denomination, our congregation.

Our unity will become a reality when we recognize the power packed in Matthew 5:20-24 proclaimed for us today. When all is said and done, to be one in the Spirit and one in the Lord, we must first reconcile with our brothers and sisters. We must first recognize our own imperfections, our own rigidity, our own inclination toward exclusivity and self-righteousness before we can offer the gift of ourselves to God and others.

The gospel passage indicates that we need to leave our gift, the present and presence we are, at the altar until we can peaceably coexist within the fabric and framework of our differences. We are being told that we cannot worship in our individual sanctuaries until and unless we have revered the sanctuary of humankind. We must leave the gift of our individual denominational stance at the altar until we are living in harmony with each other. That's a scary thought. It's also exciting. It fills us with enthusiasm in the deepest sense of that word.

Can you imagine what would or could happen in the greater Shallotte area if everyone from every church community, every church family, would leave their familiar sanctuaries to gather in the street in a movement of reconciliation? Can you see the crowds of people? I can see them. They are hugging each other with inspirited love. They are whispering words of reverence and awe, phrases that offer apology and accept forgiveness. Probably the most common ones would be expressed in these words, "I didn't know."

I didn't know that your beliefs and mine are more alike than they are different. I didn't know that our becoming one doesn't mean that I have to be identical to you. I didn't realize that we are both striving to have God at the center of our lives. I didn't know that unity includes diversity. I am sorry that I concentrated on denominational differences instead of our commonality in faith.

Now we can go back to our sanctuaries pick up the gifts we left behind and offer them with renewed faith, deepened hope, and intensified charity to God who gave them to us in the first place. Now we can worship separately in the style to which we have become accustomed, knowing that we are one in heart and mind. We have been released from all that held us in bondage, separated one from the other. We have paid the last penny, given to God the last vestige of our desires.

Our heart, our very being, has been broken open. We are free. We are one. We can now devote ourselves to the teaching of the apostles and to the communal life, to the breaking of the bread, and to the prayers.

2012

What Are You Doing Here?
1 KINGS 19:9-18

Rhonda Blevins
Tellico Village Community Church

Oh my. When God asks a question, watch out! To Elijah, God asks a question not once, but twice. "What are you doing here, Elijah?" Watch out, Elijah. God isn't done with you yet. So the story goes something like this. Our hero, Elijah, is running for his life from the villainous Queen Jezebel. You may remember what happened on Mt. Carmel. Jezebel led the Israelites in the way of Baal worship. She killed off many of the Lord's prophets, so Elijah confronted her husband, King Ahab, and told him to assemble all the prophets of Baal together for a dual to the end, so to speak, so that the people of Israel would choose once and for all who they would worship. So King Ahab assembled 450 prophets of Baal together on Mt. Carmel. On two separate altars, two bulls would be placed. They would call on their respective gods to set fire to the altar. Whichever God responded, that would be the God Israel would worship. So the prophets of Baal went first. They danced. They prayed. They shouted, "Answer us!" Nothing. Morning came and went. Nothing. Through the midday. Nothing. Then evening fell. Nothing. Then it was Elijah's turn-the lone prophet of Yahweh. The bull was placed upon the altar in much the same way. But he added a little twist. He poured twelve large jars of water over the sacrifice, just for a little drama. He prayed. The fire of the Lord fell. The people rejected Baal and offered their worship to Yahweh. Then Elijah had the 450 prophets of Baal slaughtered-just for good measure. Well, Jezebel didn't take too kindly to her prophets being killed, so she sent a text message to Elijah saying she would have his head on a platter. She was just the kind of woman to keep her promise. So Elijah ran for his life. 40 days and 40 nights, until he found a cave at Mt. Horeb. Scared, tired, alone, he spent the night in that cave, and that's we find him in today's lection. Hiding out in a cave.

Do you ever feel like Elijah? Do you ever feel like hiding out in a cave? Every now and then, doesn't it feel like Jezebel's minions are after you, trying to kill you, and you simply want to find a safe place, far away from your troubles, and hide out? Now, Elijah was no coward. Mt. Carmel proved that. No, he was anything but yellow. But sometimes, like for Elijah, it seems that we fight and we fight and eventually we're all out of fight. We just want to run away and hide. And if what the poet said is true-there is a time for everything-then certainly there is a time for hiding. When threats are real. When mental and physical health are at stake. When healing is needed. There is a time for hiding and there is a time to come out of hiding. That's when the Lord says, "What are you doing in here?" Did you notice the pity party Elijah offered as an answer? "Nobody likes me. Everybody hates me. And it's all your fault, God." So God showed Elijah a little something. Not in the wind. Not in the earthquake. Not in the fire. Not in any of the usual ways God showed up in theophanies. No, God came in the silence. But Elijah missed it. God asked again, "What are you doing here?" Elijah, having missed God's self-revelation, repeated his same old whine: "Nobody likes me. Everybody hates me. And it's all your fault." All this finger-pointing didn't seem to faze God. (God is used to that, you know.) Ignoring Elijah's complaint, God simply tells him, "Hey Elijah, move along. I've got a job for you to do. Come out of the cave, Elijah. I'm not done with you yet."

I get this story. I get it more than ever before, this week. I've read this story many times. I've even preached it a time or two. But this week, I felt like Elijah, wanting nothing more than to hide out in a cave, far, far away from everyone and everything. It was just one of those terrible, horrible, no-good, very-bad weeks. Has anyone ever had a week like that? A week where nothing seemed to go right? My cat got sick-had to take her to the vet. A bill came due that I wasn't expecting. I burned myself getting something out of the oven (I know! I was surprised to learn I had one too!) And to top it all off, someone hurt my feelings. (Awwwww.) By Thursday, I was ready to crawl off into a cave with a good book, a cup of coffee, and have myself a humdinger of a pity-party. And I did for about a day. But then God reminded me, "Hey Blevins. Move along. I've got a job for you to do." You see, my name was right there on the preaching lineup. All I wanted to do was feel sorry for myself, but God had a word for the people. "Come out of the cave, Rhonda. I'm not done with you yet." Well, here I am. I guess God isn't done with me yet. And God isn't done with *us* yet.

You know this story about Elijah is so remarkable because it seems that he goes from the highest of the high to the lowest of the low. From brazen, victorious, and strong on Mt. Carmel in one scene to fearful, defeated, and weak on Mt. Horeb. There's quite a striking resemblance to our church right now. Back in December, we opened the doors to this beautiful new sanctuary. The result of tremendous sacrifice of time, talent, and treasure of so many of you. When I think about all that went into this incredible accomplishment, I am simply dumbfounded. You did an absolutely amazing thing. God will be honored here for untold decades. Future generations of Christians will marvel at what you've done together.

103

What an incredible feat! But I wonder if the elation of December has given way to the doldrums of August. The victory on Mt. Carmel has left us weary and tired. It's tempting to feel as if our work is now done. But God have mercy on us if we built this beautiful sanctuary just so that we'd have a bigger cave to hide in! Can you hear God now? "Hey church! Move along. I've got a job for you to do!" You remember me saying, "There's a time for hiding and a time to come out of hiding?" "Come out of the cave, Community Church! I'm not done with you yet." God's not done with me. God's not done with us. And God's not done with *you.*

I've got a friend who serves as a pastor in metro Atlanta-kind of a rough part of town the way he describes it. A while back, this homeless man stood outside when church would let out on Sunday mornings, asking for money. Well, some folks gave him some money, so guess what happened the next week. He was back, asking for more money. This went on for a while, and some folks from the church befriended him. They learned his name was Mike. They invited Mike to church-they made him feel welcomed. They showed him love and friendship. Eventually, Mike was baptized and became a member of that church. My pastor friend was so proud of his people for being the presence of Christ in Mike's life. Not too long after Mike's baptism, my friend was at home with his family in the church parsonage, when there came a knock at the door. It was Mike. What do you think was my friend's assumption? He thought Mike was there for a handout. That wasn't the case at all. Instead, Mike handed my friend a plastic bag filled with coins. Mike was offering his tithe to the church-10% of what he had collected on the street that week. My friend's first instinct was to decline the gift, knowing that Mike needed those coins more than the church needed them. He quickly thought better and accepted the gift, knowing that it was important to demonstrate the worth-the inherent value-of Mike's gift. You see, Mike had something important to offer. If Mike, one of the "least of these" has something important to offer, what does that mean for you and for me? There's not a single person here who doesn't have some kind thing to do, some healing word to say, some good gift to give. But we're kind of like the people in that show, "Hoarders." We keep our deeds, our compliments, and our gifts stored away in our caves, as if they'll do us any good in there. "Come out of the cave, my child! I'm not done with you yet."

Back to our scripture lesson. Elijah was obedient to the Lord's prompting. He found the young Elisha and invested him with the prophetic office. He spent the rest of his earthly life, some 7 or 8 years, mentoring him and quite literally walking with him in the journey. Those 7 or 8 years paid off. Elisha served the Lord as a prophet to Israel for roughly 60 years, long after Elijah's whirlwind trip to heaven. Job well done, Elijah. Time well spent. Much better than hanging out with a bunch of bats.

When God asks a question, watch out! When God asked Elijah "What are you doing here?", it quickly led to "Come out of the cave. I'm not done with you yet!" So I close with a time of silence, following all the noise. In this moment of silent reflection, I invite that same question to resonate within you. "What are you doing here?

TRUE WORSHIP

JOHN 4:4-30

R. Tim Meadows
*Associate Pastor, Tellico Village
Community Church
Loudon, Tennessee*

I guess I'll see you in about three weeks," snapped the grumpy old man, to no one in particular and really to everyone around him who might listen. It seems that this grumpy old man had just gained knowledge of the fact that his rather formal church would be experimenting with some different worship styles in the weeks to come and that, in fact, the week to follow after the beautiful classical service that he had just enjoyed, he would be subjected to contemporary worship. And the week following that, he would be subjected to bluegrass music in worship. And so to no one in particular and to everyone who would listen, he snapped, "I guess I'll see you in about three weeks."

As a veteran of the worship wars who's heard that and much worse in the years that I've served churches, I take some comfort in the fact that Jesus also dealt with this same sort of thing, that Jesus also confronted those who weren't quite sure about how worship was supposed to look, and then confronted others who were exactly sure how worship was supposed to look, who were fairly certain that the way anyone else was doing it was not correct. Yes, Jesus dealt with this same sort of thing, and the passage that you just heard from the Gospel of John shows us how Jesus dealt with the question of the proper location of worship.

In dealing with this woman who was very concerned about the proper location of worship, Jesus simply declared that worship, in fact, is not about location. It's not about style. It's not about dress. It's not about music. It's not about formality versus informality. But, Jesus declared, worship is about the heart; real worship comes from a heart of spirit and truth.

As often happens with Jesus (I don't know whether to blame this on Jesus or to blame it on the gospel writers, but if I ever find out I'll let you know who's at fault), Jesus makes this declaration about spirit and truth and then stops. And we're not told how to discern whether one is worshiping in spirit and in truth. But there are some indications in Scripture and from life that we can examine to help us determine whether or not our hearts worship in spirit and in truth.

For the next few minutes, I want to invite you on that journey. Let me begin by suggesting to you that one of the ways that I think we can evaluate the spirit and truth of worship is through our acts of charity. After all, Jesus does say that the eternal value of our lives will be judged on how well we fed the hungry, how well we clothed the naked, how well we cared for the poor, how often we visited those who were imprisoned. And in the letter attributed to Jesus' brother, James tells us in fact that pure religion or true religion approved by God is the kind of religion that makes certain that those on the margins of life are always cared for. James speaks specifically of caring for the widows and the orphans and those for whom no one else in society would find concern. So maybe, just maybe, these are some of the measures of spirit and truth in worship. If we want to know whether our hearts are indeed engaged in spirit and truth, we can look at our acts of charity.

So I ask you today: if Jesus were to look at your acts of charity, would he find the spirit and truth of worship?

I would also suggest that a way of evaluating the spirit and truth of worship is through our stands of courage in life. Let me tell you a couple of stories.

The first story is about a friend who grew up in middle Georgia when the issues of segregation were about to reach a boiling point. This friend left work one day and went as he normally did to public transportation and got on the bus and sat down with an empty seat beside him. Not too long after he sat in the empty seat, an older African American gentleman also entered the bus. As he was standing there weary from his day of work, my friend said to him, "Sir, why don't you sit down?" The gentleman began to protest, "Son, you know the rules. You know how life is here. You know that I can't sit there. You know that's not legal." To which my friend said, "Well, I'm sitting here, and this seat is empty, and I think I can invite anyone to sit beside me that I'd like. And I'm inviting you to sit down. So, why don't you sit down?" The elderly gentleman decided with an invitation like that he probably should respond to the young man. He sat down.

You can imagine in middle Georgia at the height of segregation that it would not be long before a big, burly, authoritative bus driver appeared and proceeded to tell the African American man that he could not sit there. "Sir, you must get up. That seat is not available to you." My young friend, full of brash energy and enthusiasm, accosted the bus driver and protested, "But I asked him to sit there, and as far as I'm concerned I can ask anyone to sit beside me that I like." You can imagine again knowing the times and conditions, the bus driver didn't wait long before he ceremoniously dumped both of these individuals off of the bus. It may have been a long walk home for my friend, but I think that kind of stand of courage exhibits the kind of spirit and truth that Jesus said was essential to our worship.

When I think of stands of courage, I also think of Congressman John Lewis from the fifth district of Georgia. Congressman Lewis has been a champion for the neglected his entire career. He has stood in the gap for things that most people said could never be legislated, could never be passed. He has worked for the oppressed and neglected and made a life doing so. But it almost didn't happen. As a young man Congressman John Lewis was almost killed. As a nonviolent freedom rider and a nonviolent protestor on the Pettus Bridge in Selma, Alabama, with Hosea Williams and others, Congressman Lewis was beaten, bloodied, and left for dead, hoping by those who beat him that his voice would be silenced. Today John Lewis' body still bears the marks of the many beatings that he took. If you ask me, these stands of courage exemplify the very spirit and truth in worship of which Jesus spoke.

So, if it is by stands of courage that we evaluate the spirit and truth of worship, let me ask you: if Jesus looked at the stands of courage you have taken in your life, would he find the spirit and truth of worship?

We can also evaluate the spirit and truth of worship through lives of character. Most of you know that I'm a huge major league baseball fan. And in fact I spend a lot of time trying to get to major league parks and to minor league parks as well. If I'm at home watching baseball, I flip between two channels with one game in the picture-in-picture and try to follow both games at the same time. For about nine months out of the year, baseball becomes my life; and, yes, the St. Louis Cardinals will win the World Series. But this year in the baseball world, it's been a bittersweet year, because this year we say goodbye to one of baseball's finest. The career of Chipper Jones is coming to an end. Everywhere that Chipper has gone all season, there have been great tributes to him by people from opposing cities and teams. They've lauded and celebrated the grand career that Chipper Jones has had. But I think the greatest tribute that I've heard Chipper receive through this year was one that was offered one night by one of the AtlantaBraves' broadcasters:

> I was talking with the Atlanta Braves historian the other day, and this is what he says about Chipper Jones:
>
> When I think of a modern player who epitomizes the game of baseball and what a modern baseball player should be, I think of Chipper Jones. Further, when I try to get a visual of what an Atlanta Brave should look like, the visual that I get is of Chipper Jones, a life of character.

I wonder, if people were seeking visuals, say in the automotive industry or in the field of engineering or in sales or banking or government service or ministry, I wonder if the visuals they would get would be of any of us.

A life of character is the measure of spirit and truth in our worship. And so I ask you, if Jesus were to look at your life of character, would he find the spirit and truth of worship?

I have to tell you, I feel sorry for that grumpy old man that I talked about earlier. I feel sorry for him because he has confused the essence of worship with style. I feel sorry for the woman in our New Testament lesson today because for far too long she confused the location of worship with the essence of worship itself. And I feel sorry for us if we don't recognize that the truth of worship is about spirit and truth, if we don't recognize that the spirit and truth to which Jesus points must arise out of our acts of charity, out of our stands of courage, and out of lives of character. If we don't recognize that, then we've missed what Jesus says is truly the heart of worship. May God give us the grace and the

110

eyes to see that this, in fact, is the kind of worship of which God approves. Amen!

2014

JESUS MIGHT BE THE ANSWER...
BUT WHAT IS THE QUESTION?
LUKE 4:14-30

Herb Freitag
Chapel By The Sea

I saw a bumper sticker the other day (one I have seen numerous times before)... and I am sure that you have also seen the same message, whether on a car or a billboard: JESUS IS THE ANSWER! Chew on that for awhile - Jesus is the answer. To those of us who are Christian, the immediate reaction might be one of agreement. .. it is only a four-word phrase but it is succinct; it is clever; it is positive; it sounds right. However, even a bit of thought must lead to the observation ... okay, but what is the question - what is the question to which Jesus is the answer? Because, I would suggest, Jesus is not the answer to every question!

A rich man once told me that he doesn't go home anymore because when he does, everyone has his or her hand out. That's kind of what happens to Jesus - he gets used over and over and over... and often the use is misuse. All kinds of claims are made for what one gets when one believes in Christ, and so many of them are neither biblical nor logical nor correct. All kinds of claims are made for what God will do for one if one has the right faith and follows the right rituals and says the right words and espouses the right beliefs... and this is done by Christians and Jews and Muslims and folks of pretty much all brands of religious observance ... but too often there is no evidence to back up such claims. All kinds of claims promising well-being are made to those who must do nothing more than accept Jesus Christ as Lord and Savior, but what such well-being might entail is often misleading and untrue.

Throughout his ministry, friends and enemies, supporters and critics, were continually trying to figure Jesus out. They flat out

112

didn't understand him. To them, he was an enigma in a paradox in a quandary - he was far more complex than he ever appeared and, besides that, they couldn't figure out why a man of his obvious power and talents would not use them as seemed most positive and productive. They loved his miracles and thought that everything he did should be miraculous. If he was the messiah, they wanted him to act like a messiah... or at least like their concept of a messiah. The result? - all too often Jesus was a disappointment to even those who loved and followed him. And they wanted so badly for him to be what they hoped and expected him to be.

I would suggest that nothing has changed, even after 2000 years. So we say that Jesus is the answer because we want Jesus to be the answer - the answer to those questions of and in life which confound and perplex us; to those problems of and in life which seem overwhelming and frequently leave us disheartened and frustrated; to those situations of and in life over which we have little if any control and in the face of which we feel helpless. We want Jesus to meet our perceived needs and wants... but sometimes our perceived needs and wants have nothing to do with what Jesus was all about.

So what was Jesus all about? - perhaps that is a place to start. Our scripture lesson of the morning provides at least a partial answer... and reading somewhat between the lines, in addition to utilizing the rest of the picture we have of him, hopefully adds to our understanding. When our episode reported in Luke occurred, Jesus had just returned from what we call his "temptation in the wilderness". During the forty days he was alone, wrestling with what he thought his mission was and how he was going to accomplish what he felt he had been called to do, Jesus had not had an easy time of it. But he came away from his ordeal with strength of mind and purpose - he knew where he was going... and believed that God had given him what he needed to succeed.

So here he was in the synagogue in his hometown after spending some time traveling around Galilee and making a name for himself as a preacher and teacher. The folks there were eager to hear what he had to say. After all, they had heard about him and had a bit of trouble connecting this image of influence and prestige because they, and they alone, are the ones needed in the political offices they hold.

When you think of the picture of Jesus presented in and by the New Testament, does all that square with what you find there? I don't think so. I'm not suggesting that politicians are never moral or ethical... but I am suggesting that Jesus doesn't care what they do for a living, although he might care about how they do the work to which they are elected. Jesus, remember, distanced himself from all political power and those who held it. He only came in contact with them when they were hurting those who were under their authority... and then it was as their adversary and critic, not as their supporter or ally. Jesus, himself, indicated time and again that his "kingdom" was a spiritual one rather than an earthly one... so he presented no plans or procedures on how to run a political campaign. So Jesus is not the answer for those asking: *How can I attain power?*

Jesus is not the answer if the question concerns national dominance. Every nation that has ever fought a war has claimed that God was on its side... and it doesn't matter what religion was dominant in that country. So a predominantly Christian nation fights in the name of Jesus and a predominantly Jewish nation fights in the name of Jehovah and a predominantly Muslim nation fights in the name of Allah... and all of them kill with the same gusto and self-righteousness in what each perceives, somehow, as a "holy war". I'm not suggesting here that war is never justified or necessary ... but I am suggesting that we leave Jesus, the "Prince of Peace", out of it. And I am also suggesting that when it comes to national preference and prominence, God doesn't play favorites - all people are his people; all families are his family. And, in some way, he blesses them all equally. What they do with those blessings might vary, but the love of God doesn't. Were you listening when I read this morning's scripture lesson? Then you remember how furious those Jews worshiping in the synagogue got with Jesus when he said that, in the past, the folks who were sometimes apparently helped by God through difficult times were not necessarily Jews!

114

And to claim that God is always on the same wavelength as Americanism or German-ism or Russian-ism or Iranian-ism or Congo-ism or any-ism has no biblical foundation - in fact, such a claim would fly in the face of what the bible does say. So Jesus is not the answer for those asking: How is my nation favored over all other nations?

There are numerous other questions to which Jesus is not the answer. Jesus is not the answer for those who see the wrongs in the world and the people who hurt others and do not attempt to do anything about any of it in the belief that Jesus, too, would have sat back and meekly accepted all that happened, good or bad, fair or unfair, just or unjust - seemingly they don't remember what he did to the temple money-changers who were bilking the poor and desperate. Jesus is not the answer for those who expect that they deserve special treatment because they behave a certain way or believe a certain way or speak a certain way - seemingly they don't remember what he said about God's sunshine and rain falling upon everyone without regard for their self-perceived goodness. Jesus is not the answer for those who think that, because they call themselves Christians, they are better than everyone else who is not a Christian, or their brand of Christian - seemingly they don't remember that Jesus was not a Christian... nor was he legalistic or ritualistic as he bent the rules, when necessary, to do the real work of God.

So to what is Jesus the answer, an answer, our answer? Jesus is our answer to those questions concerning how one should live in keeping with what Jesus, at least, perceived as the will of God. And Jesus is our answer to those questions concerning how one can attain a clearer picture of the divine and gain some guidance on how to form a closer relationship with God. And Jesus is our answer to those questions concerning how lives can be changed for the better in terms of caring and compassion, of dedication and discipleship, of sacrifice and service, of faith and fortitude. And Jesus is our answer to those questions concerning how to acquire the strength to overcome such problems as worthlessness and despondency, of loneliness and despair. And Jesus is our answer to those questions concerning the possibility of eternal life. And Jesus is our answer to those questions concerning how one can and why one should become, as much as possible, like him. Like him?

> *The Spirit of the Lord is upon me, because he has anointed me to bring good news to the poor. He has sent me to proclaim release to the captives and recovery of sight to the blind, to Jet the oppressed go free, to proclaim the year of the Lord's favor.*

Jesus might be the answer... but what is the question?

2015

We Believe. In You.
I PETER 2:4-10

William F. Schnell
May 18, 2014

Has anyone ever discovered that you are a church member? Have you ever been asked about the kind of church you attend? Have you ever encountered clarifying questions when you said you attended "The Church in Aurora?" Questions like: "Which church in Aurora?" Have you ever noticed a certain perplexity when you said that you attended a Community Church? Were you asked, "What do they believe?" or "How do they worship?"

I get those same questions by clergy of other denominations. According to the last count the Ohio Council of Churches is comprised of 17 Catholic, Orthodox and Protestant denominations representing six thousand Ohio congregations and three million Ohio worshipers. Somehow I ended up being President of that organization, which may be a dismal commentary on the state of ecumenism in Ohio today. But one of the blessings of that experience has been regular contact with the judicatory heads of the various faith traditions in Ohio—primarily referred to as bishops, such as Bishop Elizabeth Eaton who last August was elevated to become the first female Presiding Bishop of the Evangelical Lutheran Church in America (name dropper alert).

Last fall I was hosted by Episcopal Bishop Mark Hollingsworth in his office suite at Trinity Cathedral in downtown Cleveland. His is a sweet suite I can tell you that. We were joined by Bishop John Hopkins of the United Methodist Church, among others. Both Bishops were keenly interested in the question of spiritual authority in Community Churches. Who owns the building, if not the diocese or conference or what-have-you? Who picks the pastor? Who determines the theology or official stance on issues?

I explained that authority of Community Churches is vested in its members. The members own the property, choose the pastor and chart the course. I could tell this seemed like a chaotic plan to them, as if such a groundless organization could quickly and easily veer off into some cultish directions (although they were polite enough not to suggest such a thing). I mentioned that the church I served had maintained an amazingly consistent identity for over two centuries—longer than 99% of congregations west of the Ohio River and a good percentage east. I was polite enough not to mention that we have thus far avoided the declining fortunes experienced by old line denominations such as theirs.

Like all Christian Churches we believe in God and in his Written Word the Bible and in his Incarnate Word Jesus. What makes us distinctive is that we connect believing in God with believing in you. We believe you are children of God no better or worse than any other regardless of denominational distinctions. We believe you are vessels of God's Holy Spirit. We believe you should have the undisturbed right to follow the Word of God according to the dictates of your own conscience. We believe you are capable of owning the building and calling the pastor. We believe. In you.

We also believe that this connection between believing in God and believing in his children is a stream of Christianity that goes way back to the beginning and is rooted in scripture. On this Community Church Sunday we are going once again bring the Bible to bear on the subject using a text which just happens to be assigned for this day by the Revised Common Lectionary. It is from Peter's first epistle, or letter, and it uses a variety of metaphors which are near and dear to him.

He writes: *As you come to him the living Stone—rejected by men but chosen by God and precious to him—you also, like living stones, are*

118

being built into a spiritual house... (Verses 4-5). Stones and rocks are a favorite image for Peter ever since Jesus gave him his nickname. His real name was Simon, but Jesus affectionately called him Petros, or Peter, meaning "rocky." When Peter confessed that Jesus was the Son of God, *Jesus replied, "Blessed are you, Simon son of Jonah, for this was not revealed to you by man, but by my Father in heaven. And I tell you that you are Peter, and on this rock I will build my church, and the gates of Hades will not overcome it* (Matthew 16:17-18).

Jesus would build his church upon living stones like Peter. Peter says: *you also, like living stones, are being built into a spiritual house*—a temple where God's Holy Spirit dwells. A temple needs priests, does it not? Here Peter switches metaphors. God's people are, as he put it, to be a holy priesthood. A little later in our text he calls God's people *a royal priesthood* (Verse 9). From this text, and others like it, the great religious reformer, Martin Luther, derived the notion of "the priesthood of all believers," but we get ahead of ourselves.

What Peter is relaying from Jesus is a radical concept for his day to the point of being illegal. Jesus and all of his original followers were Jews. They belonged to the institutional religious establishment of their day. There was the temple in Jerusalem, and synagogues elsewhere. There was a religious hierarchy from the High Priest to the scribes and teachers of the Law. There were religious parties like the Sadducees and Pharisees. It was a clearly defined system and it did not take well to the likes of Jesus.

Jesus interpreted scriptures differently and acted upon them differently. "By what authority" the religious establishment wanted to know? Worst of all his preaching and teaching so resonated with the people that he threatened the whole system. Something had to be done about Jesus. It was the religious establishment that drug him before the Roman authorities and clamored for his crucifixion when even the Roman Governor, Pilate could find nothing against him.

Jesus is the classic religious reformer who wrests authority from "the authorities" and gives it back to the people—common people like a fisherman named Simon, a tax collector named Matthew and so forth. "The authorities" try to stamp out his band and his brand but they cannot. It is a spiritual reformation whose time has come. Even the foremost persecutor of the early Christian Church, named Saul, converts and becomes the new faith's chief evangelist (renamed Paul).

In time even a Roman Emperor named Constantine converts to Christianity. The downside is that the Church becomes institutionalized again with a basilica in Rome named after Rocky, er, St. Peter. A whole hierarchy develops including religious orders and priests and bishops and archbishops and cardinals and a supreme bishop in Rome known as the pope. Traditions build upon traditions. The bigger it becomes the more confusing it becomes for the common lay person. And eventually abuses creep in.

Enter again a priest named Martin Luther. He begins that most heretical of all pastimes: questioning. Where in the Bible is there anything about granting indulgences for instance? If you had a loved one who died and you were concerned about that loved one's status in the hereafter, you could ensure forgiveness of sins by purchasing an indulgence from the Church. Indeed, if you had your own share of sins needing forgiveness, just purchase the occasional indulgence. What a racket for the religious powers-that-be.

The only problem, according to Luther, is that the practice had absolutely no biblical foundation. The common folks did not have any way of knowing that because the Bible was literally chained to the pulpit for the exclusive use of the clergy. And just in case there were any prying fingers and sneaky eyes, it was written in the Latin language that nobody but the clergy was trained to read. But Martin Luther was a priest trained in Latin and he read the Bible and he began to question certain practices.

For that he was branded a heretic and condemned to capital punishment. Sound familiar? Once again we have a religious reformation whose time had come. All of a sudden the Bible is illegally translated into the language of the people and distributed and studied by common folks. All of a sudden religious protesters separate from the established church to start their own Protestant churches. All of a sudden whole countries establish state churches of their own.

The Church of England separates from Rome when Henry VIII requests an annulment from Catherine of Aragon to marry Anne Boleyn. Unfortunately the pope is concerned about what Catherine's nephew will think, who happens to be the Roman Emperor in the castle next door. As a result, Henry establishes The Church of England where the Supreme Head is, you guessed it, the King himself. He grants himself an annulment and marries Anne. As you may also have guessed, abuses begin to enter The Church of England.

Some try to purify the church from within, known as Puritans. Others feel the situation is hopeless and separate from the church, known as Separatists. Eventually King James (of King James Bible fame) declares: "I will make them conform themselves, or else I will harry them out of the land, or else do worse." Some separatists get the point and head out on the Mayflower for Plymouth Rock. There they establish Congregational Churches—churches which are congregationally owned and operated.

As civilization spreads west, so do the Congregationalists. A church is established in a wilderness outpost called Aurora, Ohio. As it is written in A History of The Church in Aurora: "The members of the first church in Aurora organized themselves under the Congregational form of government. Churches in this category were self-governing. Congregations selected their own pastor and elected their own church officers. No church hierarchy had authority over them."

"The rest," as they say, "is history." It is history repeating itself over and over again in terms of religious reformation. It is a return to what the Protestants called "the priesthood of all believers," and what Peter called a royal priesthood. It is the freedom to worship God, not according to the dictates of a king, or the dictates of a bishop or the dictates of a Pharisee or the dictates of any external authority; but according to the dictates of conscience as each is led by the Holy Spirit.

We respect the freedom of others to believe in the pope, or a protestant bishop, or denominational dogma. They believe in God their way, and we respect that. We believe in God too. We believe in a God who has a long history of speaking through the voice of his people, often over and against the religious institutions of their day as did Jesus Christ. Jesus believed in everyone from mongrel Samaritans to the worst of sinners—that they had potential to be saints. We believe in Jesus. We Believe. In You.

2016

Words Fail, Love Wins
ROMANS 8: 18 – 39

By Rev. Dr. Joe Sellepack

Have you ever had a moment when words fail you? It may be something beautiful, so deeply touching that you had a speechless moment when the right words to describe the event were just not there. Words might've failed at the birth of your son or daughter, your first kiss, or the moment when you first saw your spouse. Words might've failed on the vacation you took to the Grand Canyon and you stood on the precipice for the first time and it took your breath away. It might've been when you witnessed the cascade of Niagara Falls for the first time. Words can fail us when the beauty and the grandeur of the moment seem so vastly superior to whatever you do to describe it. Even the photos or the selfies that we snap don't do them justice. Words fail...

Then there are other moments when words fail that aren't so good. The event causes you to feel numb and the grief, sadness, or anxiety is so real that it socks you in the gut. Unable to catch your breath, you are just trying to get through it. Words fail...

Words can be limiting. I might tell you the word table and you may have in your mind a rectangle, Formica covered, chrome legs and trim, and vinyl covered chairs. Or you might be thinking of that round table you grew up with that was made of oak with all of the grooves cut into it from countless meals and homework assignments. Table means many things to many people. Just using the word table is not nearly enough. Words fail...

The limitation of words to communicate reminds us that sometimes we are powerless to choose the right one to express how we are feeling or what we are thinking. Sometimes the experience takes time to process. In my mind I can picture an experience as if it had just happened. I replay it in my mind and think about what I actually said and slap myself in the head because now given distance and perspective that comes with time I know how I should have responded or what I should've said. The perfect word becomes obvious and I wish I had a do over button that would bring me back in time and relive the moment and say the right word. Words fail…

I remember when my nephew Michael died. It was two years ago this past August and he was severely injured during a diving accident. He came up out of the ocean and was waiting to be picked up by the diving boat. Somehow, freakishly, while he waited he breathed in some water. He pulled himself into the boat alright and sat down. He then found it hard to breath, passed out, and according to the doctor who was fortunately diving with him that day, Mikey then went into cardiac arrest. The doctor immediately started CPR and tried to resuscitate him. While he was able to restore his heart beat, Mikey never regained consciousness.

The extended family gathered to be with Mikey and his immediate family. We spent hours reading to him and talking with him and rubbing his hands and feet. For a week we waited until the doctors could do a brain flow test to see if he had any function in his brain. That day came, and they did the test. While we waited for the results my wife Shelly and I went into the room to read Mikey his favorite book, "Hitchhiker's Guide to the Galaxy." While we were reading my brother and his wife walked into the room. All I had to do was look at them and I knew that they had received the report from the doctor and the results weren't good. I hugged my brother and we cried together, numb is the description I would give how I felt at the moment. Then I walked out into the waiting room and my son – my 230 pound football player – came to me and put his head in the crook of my neck and sobbed. Words failed…

I am glad at moments like that that there are groans which God can decipher. God knows that all of the creation has been in labor. We know the pain, the travail, the sweat, the blood, the gore of what goes on in childbirth. According to Romans that is where we are at the present time. We don't know the joy of the release that comes when the baby is born, we're in the between time when the struggle to give birth is real and the groans are all that escape our mouths.

God knows that as humans our lives can change in a heartbeat. One moment we can be on the top of the world at the height of our game. Everything seems to be going our way and one success leads to another. But then the doctor delivers the test results and it floors you. He uses words like cancer, stroke, heart disease, or aneurysm. The world shifts under your feet and you know, you just know, that words fail…

And maybe that's as is should be. At moments like those it is important to realize that words fail, not because we don't have to have the right words to express our thoughts. No, it's not that we are simply at a loss for words, or too immature to express the right word, or that we are not wise enough to know a phrase to fill the silence. No, at moments like those the right words just don't exist. All we can do at moments like those is groan and tears become the only response that makes sense. Words fail…

But according to Romans, somehow the desire to communicate must give way to the desire to trust in the relationship and find love in the silence. We need to know that there is a God who undergirds all of our experiences. Because this God is with us, beyond the suffering of the present moment lays a hopeful love that is so much larger than we can possibly comprehend. The miracle is that according to Romans, when words fail, love wins.

"What can separate us from the love of God?" is the question on the lips of the writer. Then he gives us a whole bunch of one word answers: trouble, hardship, persecution, or famine, or nakedness, or danger, or sword. Then the writer pretends that the questions are merely rhetorical and gives us the apparent one word answer. No, and then pens these words, "For I am convinced that neither death nor life, neither angels nor demons, neither the present nor the future, nor any powers, neither height nor depth, nor anything else in all creation will be able to separate us from the love of God that is in Christ Jesus our Lord." In short, he wants us to know that love wins.

Love wins when words fail us. Can cancer separate us from the love of God? Can the death of children separate us from the love of God? Can the loss of our health or the development of chronic disease? Can divorce separate us from the love of God? Can the loss of our job or long term unemployment? Can chronic mental health issues separate us from the love of God? Can the foreclosure of a house? Can the loss of clout or being fired from a job? What is the worst word that you can think of, what is the one thing that you don't think you could ever survive? Think it right now. What is it? Can that word separate you from the love of God?

The answer is No. Why? Because love wins! Love wins because it is the foundation upon which the world turns. We may think that money makes the world go round but we would be wrong. We may think that power makes the world go round. We might think that oil is the answer to our problems. Health, wealth, fortune and fame all give us temporary joys, but in the end their promise is only one word away from being turned upside down. But can an economic downturn separate us from the love of God? Can it? No, it can't because we know that love wins.

Here is the good news. You are loved by a love that is so immeasurable and intense and incomprehensible that words will fail to describe it. When words fail us, God's love will see us through. Love wins.

Gordon Cosby, the founding pastor of Church of the Savior, writes, "In the struggle to become Christ's Body, we have but one weapon and one alone: Love. Any other weapon betrays the cause. We are not allowed demanding, controlling power. We are not given the power to fix things. No violence, No Hatred. Just Love.

"We have to love. We have to love those who pervert our message and even kill us. We have to love God's possibility alive in each one, even within the enemy. We have to love the beauty that is captured in each person.

"Only love. Love, love, love, scandalous love. Love like that of the Lamb slain from the foundations of the world.

"Love is what first softened your heart and mine. Love brought us into the struggle to live. Love alone has the power to break hearts open so that we will all lay down our defenses and join in the cosmic movement toward a new heaven, a new earth, in a Holy City whose foundation is Love." In short, Gordon Cosby wants us to know that Love wins…

The picture of God's love that I have in my mind comes from a book. That book is <u>Mortal Lessons</u> written by Dr. Richard Selzer. In this passage he describes an interaction between a young husband and his wife. He writes, "I stand by the bed where a young woman lies, her face postoperative, her mouth twisted in palsy, clownish. A tiny twig of the facial nerve, the one to the muscles of her mouth, has been severed. She will be like this from now on. The surgeon had followed with religious fervor the curve of her flesh; I promise you that. Nevertheless, to remove the tumor in her cheek, I had to cut the little nerve.

"Her young husband is in the room. He stands on the opposite side of the bed and together they seem to dwell in the evening lamplight, isolated from me, private. Who are they, I ask myself, he and this wry mouth I have made, who gaze at and touch each other so generously, greedily?

"The young woman speaks. "Will my mouth always be like this?" she asks. "Yes," I say, "it will. It is because the nerve was cut." She nods and is silent. But the young man smiles. "I like it," he says, "it is kind of cute."

"All at once I know who he is. I understand and lower my gaze. One is not bold in an encounter with a god. Unmindful, he bends to kiss her crooked mouth and I am so close I can see how he twists his own lips to accommodate to hers, to show her that their kiss still works."

For better or worse, God's love will stick with us. Like the young husband who kisses his wife's lips to prove that his love will not fail, God's love sticks with us. Though our lips are twisted with pain, though our lips will never be the same again, though life has dealt us a low blow and we fail to have the words to express how we feel, God's love will stick with us.

God was with us when we were born. God was with us when we were baptized. God was with us when we were confirmed. God was with us when we were married. God was with us when our children were born. God was with us when we were sick. God was with us when we got the news we didn't want to hear. God was with us when we cried and words failed us. God was with us when our pride was hurt and we failed to love each other as we should. God was with us in the best of times and in the worst of times. God was with us in the greatest accomplishments of our lives and when we took a risk and failed. God was with us then, God is with us now, and God will be with us when we one day pass through death's door into eternal love and joy. We must trust in that loving presence and know that when words fail, love wins. It always will because love is stronger than death. Thanks be to God.

2017

God's Table is Inclusive of All Peoples
ISAIAH 55:1-3

Ella Clay
Historic First Community Church, Nashville, Tennessee
MTS candidate at Vanderbilt University Divinity

In the book of Isaiah we find the words of the Lord giving an invitation to those who are in need of salvation and restoration. The Israelites are at the end of their exile from the Babylonian captivity and are in need of redemption. Being acquainted with poverty the Israelites are thirsty, hungry, and destitute. The effects of having no money or material possessions inflicted undue burdens causing the Israelites to suffer shame, shunning and desolation. While scarcity and poverty was a way of life for the ancient people, they received a clarion call by God. The call was to everyone who was thirsty and hungry to come to the water. The call to come to the water denotes abundance. This abundance indicates not merely water but strength, cheerfulness, nourishment, and spiritual blessings from God. Everyone who thirsts and hungers will have the opportunity to receive all that one needs. In other words, wherever there is lack, God calls for all to come so that we may be filled. The Israelites were given an opportunity of being fully accepted by coming to a table. The same opportunity is available to us; we too, can come to a table of full acceptance.

Can you imagine being an individual that resides in a country that is rich with money and resources, yet finding oneself living in an impoverished state? This is the case for many who reside in the United States of America. Just as the Israelites experienced Babylonian captivity, numerous individuals are suffering from the bondage of America's Babylonian captivity. Many are living in bondage within the borders of the United States of America. Daily people are confronted with being thirsty, hungry, and destitute due to lack of economics, education, healthcare, and material wealth. Although many get up and go to work every day, they are still considered the working poor. They receive unfair wages and are not able to experience a life of abundance. Often they sleep in their cars at night because they are unable to afford proper housing for themselves and their children. Some are still saddled with high cost mortgages and struggle to recover from the subprime lending. Economic exploitation and social exclusion are prevalent among education, healthcare, and jobs. The systemic systems of oppressions are so deeply embedded in the fabric of society that it becomes the status quo for humanity. The system of capitalism finds it expedient to reduce humanity to a state of enslavement. Some people often serve as a scapegoat for the evils of the system. As a result, families experience shame, shunning, and feel that they have been abandoned by all. Their overwhelming burdens leave them in despair, causing them to thirst and hunger for justice. Unfortunately, many individuals think they are the cause of their economic deficiency. They do not understand society's systemic institutional systems have created forces to perpetuate cycles of oppression.

Just as the Israelites were oppressed by the Babylonian system, many are marginalized among Western civilizations system of capitalism. The demonic force of American Babylonian captivity deprives many of economic justice and emotional stability. Their God-given rights to come to the water to receive abundance oftentimes are revoked by systemic structures. The text states, we all can come to the water whether we have money or not. If we are thirsty, we can come to the water. If we are hungry, we can come to the water. If we are spiritually bankrupt, we can come to the water to receive nourishment and spiritual blessings from God. For whosoever drinks of the water that Jesus gives will never thirst. Indeed, the water that Jesus gives will become in them a spring of water welling up to eternal life.

The text calls us to listen to God and eat what is good, and delight yourself in rich food. Incline your ear, and come to me; listen so that you may live and I will make an everlasting covenant to David. Could it be that we are not listening to God? Listening does not only mean to hear but to discern, perceive, and submit. Are we submitting to God's call to speak against injustices toward humanity? Or, are we compliant with institutional systems because some of us are living well?

Are we inclining our ears to God's earnest attention? This inclining means to bend or yield. As we incline our ears to God, we will bend or yield toward the well - being of humanity. By inclining our ears to God, we can hear as God calls us to assist our brothers and sisters. Anyone with ears to hear should listen and understand. As we listen and understand, we will see the needs of others and give nourishment that strengthens and enliven humanity. God's table is inclusive of all peoples. All humanity has the opportunity of coming to the table so that all can fair sumptuously. God desires for us to delight in spiritual and earthly blessings.

The Politics of Jesus, by Obery M. Hendricks, shares strategies Jesus used as He fought against the injustices and oppressions of others. Jesus treated people's needs as holy. As we treat our neighbors needs as holy, we strive to fulfill their needs as if we are serving God. By giving voice to the voiceless we can expose the workings of oppression. As we expose the workings of oppression, God's grace is equally distributed regardless of when or how one has come before God's throne. To call a demon by name is to call out the exploitation and oppression of others. Saving our anger for the mistreatment of others will motivate us to transform the social and political order for fair and equitable distribution of humanity. For individuals who are educationally, economically, politically, and socially deprived, the taking of blows without returning them allows us to exercise our power over abusive political systems. As Christians we don't just explain the alternative, we show it by demonstrating a new way of living in an unreserved allegiance to the Kingdom of God by bringing water and food to those who are in need.

131

As believers, our collective desire should be for all to fare well economically, emotionally, educationally, materially, and spiritually. The responsibilities of Christians are to be concerned for the needs of others. Jesus calls us to love the Lord God with all of our hearts, and with all of our souls, and with all of our minds, and we shall love our neighbors as we love ourselves. We should not want our sisters and brothers to be thirsty or hungry. Doing justly, loving mercy, and walking humbly before God and humanity should be our interest. Our faith compels us to repent of the injustices and oppressions that are inflicted upon the marginalized. Isaiah 55: 7 (NRSV) states, "Let the wicked forsake their way, and unrighteous their thoughts let them return to God, for he will abundantly pardon."

There is a great divide among class and economics in the United States. I am reminded of my field placement service. The evidence of thirst and hunger was throughout a community where I served. As I toured the community there was a sense of depression, hopelessness, and death. It appeared that the community was not aware of God's clarion call for those who were thirsty and hungry. As I engaged a resident she shared that when her granddaughters were younger they were excited about their lives and desired to graduate from college and become successful.

However, because of their economic, psychological, spiritual, social, and political thirst, they were no longer enthusiastic about their futures. They lost their hopes, goals, and dreams due to the existing disparities. I consider that the systemic systems of economics, social and political oppressions have adversely affected the girls. The institutional structures have caused them to feel ashamed, shunned, and abandoned. The grandmother spoke about death being rampant throughout the community. She felt overwhelmed by the community's environment.

Nevertheless, as God displayed faithfulness to the Israelites by allowing them to come to a table of abundance, God offers restoration to this community. God offers salvation and restoration to all the oppressed. As we continue to assist in various communities, we are exemplifying God's love, care and concern for humanity. By

132

covenanting with various communities, we are covenanting with God.

We all have parched areas in our lives. There are areas in all of us that are desirous for God's thirst-quenching power. The text is explicitly inclusive for all to partake in God's abundance. Even as God made a covenant with David and others, God's everlasting covenant is available to you and me.

Let us pray. Most gracious God, we praise you for your everlasting covenant. We thank you for helping us hear and attend to the cries of others. Let us not walk by and think that it is someone else's responsibility to respond to their thirst and hunger. Give us the wherewithal to attend to their needs. Help us to see our sisters and brothers as you see them. Give us courage and strength to fight against injustices and oppressions and allow restoration take place within our hearts, homes, and communities.

In Jesus name we pray. Amen.

2018

EMBRACE

Genesis 17:1-16 (*NRSV*); Psalm 22 ; Romans 4:13-25; Mark 8:31-38

Karen Neely
Norris Religious Fellowship
Norris, TN.

In the story of Sisyphus, (is that name familiar to you?) Sisyphus, pushes a boulder uphill only to watch it roll back to the bottom. He is punished to eternally suffer this task and this heavy stone. All day, every day, he struggles with the heaviness, the pain, and the futility. Albert Camus writes about Sisyphus and his incessant toil, calling it absurd. However, he looks carefully at the moment when the rock is released to roll back down the hill. He examines the footsteps as Sisyphus walks back down the hill. Camus dares to imagine Sisyphus happy in his torment; the freedom, the relief, the knowing the rock is waiting at the bottom. He wrote, "There is but one world. Happiness and the absurd are two sons of the same earth. They are inseparable. It echoes in the wild and limited universe of man". Even though we each have our boulder to accompany us, (or as Christians say, their cross to bear), our internalized suffering co-habitates in a world where there is Sun and sky, the sound of rain, and the peeps of frogs.

In this February Spring that we're having, we witness... life, living, moving outside. Norris seems to be alive with field sports and strollers and bikes. Games of soccer pop up on the Commons or people throw a ball to one another. The walking paths are active. I see whole families out. If you have been down to Songbird Trail it's a little more crowded than usual. The weather brings people out.

And yet ...at the center of it all, we have a heavy-laden river and Norris Dam, like mighty outstretched arms, holding back a full reservoir. The trees around the Clinch look to be drowning. The fullness, the passing clouds, the off/on rain are representative of something. We don't like to think about it. We'd rather focus on the clarity, the sense of newness and a change of season.

The thing we don't like to think about. Our grief. Our loss. They are no less heavy. For many, a change of season, or seeing a wildflower, represents a reminder; a mark. And if someone has that reminder, they often feel obligated to push grief-related reminders down, or at the very least, hide it until they're alone. We have ways of "protecting" by not showing grief while at work, not shedding tears in front of children, holding back emotions in classrooms and in places where we shop. So many will wait until they're alone. No one can understand *your* loss. Whether the death of a beloved or surviving some other tragedy. Your grief experience is your own. In the midst of all the Spring-like weather and yellow daffodils, it's still going to be there, often invisible. Grief and loss are there like the river, winding its way through our lives. Grief, its steady presence in the valley, like the river, is a reminder of the life-giving thing we have lost: A relationship, a loved one, a home or sense of belonging. When we lose something life-giving we grieve.

In our Gospel we have something very clear about someone wishing to avoid loss, someone adamantly attempting to stand in the way of that swollen river. Like a diagnosis, Jesus shares the news of His future. The truth embedded in The Plan. He speaks of suffering and of victory. Peter only hears suffering. Imagine your friend that you love like a sibling, imagine your greatest most beloved teacher, says something that sounds outlandish, impossible, and horribly tragic. This is more than something like going over Niagara Falls in a barrel. This is unthinkable. To quote Mark Twain, "It ain't those parts of the Bible that I can't understand that bother me, it is the parts that I do understand". Professor Black of Princeton Theological says, "There is little in this teaching that requires deep-sea exegesis. It's plain, hard, and inescapable". Peter reacts with such rejection. He is not rejecting his beloved Jesus. Peter is rejecting pain. Peter is rejecting loss. Rejecting anything about this plan that sounds insane. He is not rejecting Love, he's rejecting what he believes Death represents: loss. The rejection itself is a disruption of the Divine plan, a disruption that Jesus calls Satan. Ha-Satan, the Disruption. He follows this by reminding all of them that this is bigger than flesh and blood, bigger than earth...this whole plan is blending the spiritual with the physical, this is the whole point, the Son of G!d existing in the world as a vessel for Spirit and leading by example. Even still, it is a terminal diagnosis He delivers and the one they want to avoid.

I met with someone this week that mentioned a spinning wheel. I thought of that as a metaphor for the life cycle, the repetitive loop. In relation to grief, the things, the moment, the words where we get stuck and spin over and over. The repetition keeps us in place like we cannot move on from that one stuck spot. It can be maddening. In the immediate days, weeks, months following a loss, a conversation, a doubt, a regret, last words spoken, are unfinished business, and they all become the unending repetition. These become the story being spun. Through that spinning we are memorizing. And memorization is how we learn. Like the song this morning of call and response, *We Are Dancing Sarah's Circle*, we listen, we repeat, and we sing together in a movement that can be emotional, it draws upon something and works together in an echo of leading and following... a dancing sound.

Our stories, our experiences, our relationships—living or in living memory—are poetry. When we are touched in a way that taps into grief, that poetry becomes a lament and often involves a Spiritual conversation. That may be in the form of prayer and may contain anger, blame, a petition and sometimes...thanks.
Professor Black summarizes the Gospel passage from Mark in this way:

> *"Christian faith is not a lifestyle choice; it is a vocation to never ending struggle.... Rejecting the Son of Man, desperately trying to save our own lives, we lose our Selves [our psyche] -- just as Jesus assured us we would in Mark 8:35-37. Only by giving ourselves to others as Jesus gave Himself for us (10:45) will we ever find ourselves."/*

When I worked as a Chaplain at the Women's and Babies Hospital, many visits were marked by acute grief. In addition to the many joys found at a baby hospital, the many passes through the lobby with balloons and wheelchairs and lots of new things and car seats...the reality of peri-and neo-natal loss could either be ignored or addressed. The team I had the privilege to work with would embrace the loss. I sat with Mothers as they held the bodies of their newborns. We had a photographer who captured images: fingers and toes, curls of the hair, the little mouths and ears. We had volunteers who were always delivering hand-made knitted caps that seemed impossibly small. Oh, having the honor to be in the room when parents were singing to, holding, bathing, and dressing their babies for the first and last time. As the Chaplain, I would sometimes go to the morgue and retrieve a blanketed bundle. Within the embrace of those blankets were the losses of dreams. Those were deeply moving experiences. We were able to allow this (to create safe space for this) after so many years of hospitals whisking away death. Infant mortality was a physical disappearance and the deep scar of an emotional wound. Embracing this, experiencing this with each patient, the meaning, relationship, and connection of a space between life and loss was (and is) profound.

There is no forgetting. Loss and grief can inadvisably be ignored, swallowed, and rejected. Or loss can be embraced as an inevitable aspect encapsulated into every life. Sisyphus had to press his body into that boulder and embrace it. I think it bears saying again. No one can understand what you have lost. Tears and feelings are allowed. They're allowed to be shed and shared in the places we call Sanctuary. We are living in a time where people don't feel safe in spaces to learn, to worship, to walk alone, to cry. We can't run out of safe spaces. We need to create and sustain them, protect them, so we can provide them.

Jesus was not here to be forgotten. He showed that Death was not the end. To try to begin to understand Him we have to lose everything. We have to be willing to experience great loss and suffer the torment of grief. That's asking a lot. Because His death is recorded and repeated. We study it as a way of understanding ourselves and making our lives align with a higher purpose. Chances are, each person has an opportunity at a time of loss and grief to attach those feelings of rejection…or embrace their Higher Power. Death becomes the answer to life and life is the answer to death in a cycle that every single one of us experiences. In so much that death, though a separation becomes a gateway to our relationships that shape our individual Spirituality. And I know it's not a fun topic but it's one we all experience. Your grief is your own. This time of Lent is the wandering in the wilderness and as we get closer and closer to Easter we approach that cycle: death into life.

Let us pray: Ancient One, in this season of Lent, we ask for an ounce of Your holy wisdom in this mystery of life, death, and resurrection. We ask for patience when faced with the saga of grief, and Your healing when faced with the pain of loss. Remind us of the Divine Element at work. Help us to embrace and hold onto Love and Light in our darkest times and guide us to be gentle with ourselves and others as we witness humans on a journey. Amen.

2019

WHEN PIGS FLY
ACTS 10:1-28

Rev. Rhonda Blevins
Chapel By The Sea
Clearwater Beach, FL.

(This sermon was adapted for my congregation from the sermon I preached at the 2018 ICCC Annual Conference.)

It occurs to me that I've been your pastor for over a year now, and I haven't told you one of my favorite stories from over 20 years in the ministry. As you might imagine, being a woman in ministry has been challenging at times, interesting at times, and downright amusing at times. When I was a Southern Baptist campus minister at the University of Georgia, we held student worship on Tuesday nights. We usually invited local pastors to preach, but one Tuesday night it was my turn to preach. After worship, James, a very sincere, devout, conservative young man came up to me and said, "Rhonda, I wasn't happy about you preaching tonight, but you did a pretty good job. Can I come see you tomorrow?" I said, "Sure!" We made an appointment. James showed up right on time. "Rhonda," he said, "I wasn't happy about you preaching last night, but you did a pretty good job." I replied, "Oh, well, thank you, I think." He went on. "My roommates and I were talking last night. You remember the Old Testament story of Balaam's donkey?" "Sure," I said. "The story where God literally spoke through a donkey, right?" He said, "Right. My roommates and I decided if God can speak through a donkey, that God could speak through a woman." After I picked by jaw up off the floor, I affirmed the young man and his willingness to evolve in faith.

Today's scripture lesson presents someone evolving in faith. The lesson finds us continuing in the book of Acts, which is the story of how the early church formed and evolved along the way. So far in our

139

journey through Acts, we've learned about Jesus ascending into heaven, and about the Holy Spirit descending upon those first believers. We've seen Peter and John preach and heal people. We've read about how the Aramaic-speaking apostles evolved, allowing the Greek-speaking Jews to be given places of leadership. We saw Stephen chosen, and then we read about his execution. We've met a guy named Saul who persecuted the church until his dramatic conversion on the road to Damascus. And today we encounter Peter, who would welcome Gentiles into this movement only when he saw pigs fly. Then in a vision, he saw pigs fly. And other "unclean" creatures. And he evolved.

Let me take a poll: how many of you are Gentiles (not Jewish)? If you raised your hand, you should give thanks that Peter saw pigs fly—enabling Peter to evolve in his views—opening the door for Gentiles like me and most of you to be a part of what we now call the church. Had this not happened, it's quite likely that this "Christian" movement would have remained a Jewish movement that fizzled out before the end of the first-century.

One remarkable thing about this story of the first Gentile to be converted to faith in Jesus Christ, is Peter's brazen law-breaking. He even names it when he tells Cornelius and his family, (paraphrased) "You know it's against the law for me (a Jew) to associate with you (a Gentile)." Which brings me to the idea:

Just because it's the law doesn't mean it's just.

God revealed this truth to Peter in a vision of flying pigs. It became crystal clear to Peter when he heard the Lord say, "What God has made clean, you must not call profane."

In what ways has God revealed to you that:

Just because it's the law doesn't mean it's just?

Last week I was in St. Louis at the annual conference of the International Council of Community Churches (ICCC), the small network of churches in which our church participates. The ICCC has a remarkable history that I was delighted to learn when I began serving an ICCC church in 2007. In my early ministry, I trained and served in the Southern Baptist Convention (SBC), which has a sad history. The story goes, before the Civil War, Baptists from the South wanted to appoint as missionaries men who held slaves. Baptists in the North were opposed to slavery and to their missionaries holding slaves. So in 1845 the Baptists from the South split and the Southern Baptist Convention was born, allowing their missionaries to be slaveholders.

The ICCC, on the other hand, formed in 1950 as a merger between black community churches and white community churches. I am told that they met in Chicago—the only place in the country they could find that would allow blacks and whites to meet together. Remember, it was 1950. "Separate but equal" was still the law of the land in a racially charged environment. So as black and white met together, the leader of the black community churches and the leader of the white community churches crossed the stage, met in the middle, and shook hands, snubbing their collective noses at the Jim Crow laws designed to keep blacks and whites separate. It was 1950. You could walk down the street and see signs that read:
- "Help wanted: white only."
- "Colored served in rear."
- "Restroom: white only."

Segregation was the law. But remember:

Just because it's the law doesn't mean it's just.

Today the ICCC remains beautifully diverse—about half of our congregations are predominantly black and half are predominantly white. When I first started attending ICCC meetings in 2008, racial division was a hot topic at the annual meetings. And while I appreciated the history of the ICCC, in 2008 I didn't see race as a relevant topic. I rolled my white, suburban eyes when the talk of

141

racial tension emerged, thinking to myself, "C'mon, ICCC. Can we find a more relevant topic?"

And then Travon Martin.
And then Michael Brown.
And then Philando Castille.
And. So. Many. More.

And then God planted an individual in my life who helped me see more clearly—Peter fell into a trance in order to evolve—I fell into a conversation. From 2015-2017 I found myself in a clergy group that met at the local HBCU (Historic Black College and University) in Louisville, Kentucky. The other white clergy and I sat under the tutelage of Rev. Dr. Kevin Cosby, pastor of a mega church and president of the HBCU. Brilliant black pastor. Cosby opened my eyes to inconvenient truths about our history—he taught me about how any gains made by blacks during reconstruction have been systemically shut down. He taught me that Papa John using the "n" word, and the faux outrage surrounding that and other events like it—it's a smokescreen. Because the real outrage is that blacks are incarcerated at more than 5 times the rate of whites in a system of mass incarceration. The real outrage is the voter suppression in black communities. The real outrage is the systemic decimation of black institutions.

Cosby helped me understand part of my own history—that I was born into the middle class because my grandfather was able to enter the Civilian Conservation Corps as a part of Roosevelt's New Deal—a program largely unavailable to black folks. This elevated him and his descendants from poverty to the middle class. Other white families became middle class because of housing developments after WWII that were largely unavailable to blacks. Those opportunities created generational wealth for white families. Not for black families.

Back to the ICCC meeting. I was invited to preach on Monday. I accepted. And in accepting the invitation to preach before these friends, I knew that I had to confess my prior ignorance. I knew that I had to admit to them that I previously thought racism was irrelevant—just a story from the history books. But that I had evolved. So I confessed my truth to them. And they were so affirming as I confessed my ignorance to them, and as I asked them to help me find the courage to speak up for racial justice. For the courage to name injustice when I see it. And now that the scales have been pulled from my eyes, I see it everywhere.

Just because it's the law doesn't mean it's just.

That was Monday.

The closing worship on Thursday of ICCC is always the youth-led worship. I went in with minimal expectations, ready to offer encouragement and support to the young people, but not expecting to get much out of it. Once again, I was wrong. (Why is this a theme here?) Throughout the worship service, 17-year-old Morgan Bakaletz composed an artistic rendering that she entitled "Rise and Resist."

Here's what Morgan wrote about the piece she drew in real time:

This piece is about social justice and injustice—where it is and where it isn't. The piece as a whole symbolizes the sun. The hands are the rays and the bottom semi-circle is the center of the sun. I chose to start the center of the sun in charcoal because this world, from a distance, is hate-filled and impoverished. But I believe that up close we can connect through kindness, shown through the honey yellow on the edges of the sun, connecting through kindness.

That drawing will soon reside here at the Chapel, as it was auctioned off, and Mr. Don Prokes from our church was so inspired by the rendering that he offered the winning bid!

During the same worship service, some of the young people performed an interpretive dance to a song by Mandisa; I haven't listened to Mandisa since she was a contestant on American Idol. As Morgan continued to draw, and the young people danced, the words of Mandisa's song pierced my cynical heart:

We all bleed the same
We're more beautiful when we come together
We all bleed the same
So tell me why, tell me why
We're divided

As the music played and the artist drew and the dancers danced—I was moved. Surprising tears welled in my eyes. The lyrics continued:

Woke up today
Another headline
Another innocent life is taken
In the name of hatred
So hard to take
And if we think that it's all good
Then we're mistaken
'Cause my heart is breaking

Later that same day, after teenagers drew and danced and sang "We All Bleed the Same," far away in Clearwater, Florida, a white man shot and killed a black man in the chest over a parking spot dispute. Another Florida "Stand Your Ground" shooting. Like Mandisa, "my heart is breaking." The song continues:

Are you left? Are you right?
Pointing fingers, taking sides
When are we gonna realize?
We all bleed the same

Just because it's the law doesn't mean it's just.

The song continues:

144

If we're gonna fight
Let's fight for each other
If we're gonna shout
Let love be the cry
We all bleed the same

When asked about the inspiration for the lyrics, Mandisa, said, "My heart was broken at the state of our country. I felt like we were all fighting against one another. We just couldn't get along." Then she quoted from scripture (2 Chronicles 7:14):

"If my people who are called by my name humble themselves, pray, seek my face, and turn from their wicked ways, then I will hear from heaven, and will forgive their sin and heal their land."

As we walk in humility, may each of us be willing to let God evolve us. Healing this great land starts with you. It starts with me.

I close with lyrics to another song, one likely familiar to you:

Let there be peace on earth, and let it begin with me.

2020

The Sound of Silence: When Even the Stones Cry Out
LUKE 19:39,40,45-48

Rev. Robert Fread
Hudson, Iowa
ICCC Clergy Special Standing
Pastor, Ripley United Church of Christ, Traer, IA.

Shhhh… Do you hear that? Listen…. Do you hear it? It's the sound of silence. (Someone should write a song about that. O wait, Simon and Garfunkel did!)

Yes, it's the sound of silence. Scientifically, is that possible? Probably, not. You know that age old question, "If a tree falls in the forest and nobody hears it, does it make a sound?" My high school science teacher taught me the answer to that question is "no". He taught that "sound" must be "heard", so when that tree falls it creates "sound waves", but until the sound waves are perceived by something or "heard", then there is no sound. So, if no one hears the tree falling then there is no sound. So scientifically, I don't think silence is a sound.

But theologically I would argue silence is a sound. Actually, silence can be deafening. Silence can testify against us. Silence can judge us. At times silence must be heard by ears of faith and acted upon by lives of faith.

Today's Scripture reading picks up at the end of Jesus' entry into Jerusalem on what we usually call Palm Sunday. The followers of Jesus are quite vocal on that day shouting their "Blessed the one who comes in the name of the Lord" (Luke 19:38) and are anything but silent. Such rowdiness by Jesus' followers brings condemnation by the Jerusalem religious authorities. Basically, they tell Jesus, "Shut your followers up!", but Jesus' response is that if his followers were silent in proclaiming the presence of God's reign in their midst, such unjust silence would cause "the stones to shout out." (Luke 19:40)

So, what do stones sound like when they cry or shout? Well I was alive in the mid 1970's during the Pet Rock craze. You might recall a man named Gary Dahl, who put rocks into cardboard boxes and sold them. Yes, and by selling a single rock in a box he became a millionaire, and the creator of the Pet Rock. Well, as a boy I had a pet rock (My parents didn't buy me one, I walked out to the street, picked up a rock and brought it into the house.) My parents loved my pet rock because it didn't require food, it didn't require trips outside, and it was quiet. Yes, quiet, with no barks or meows, just silence. So, what do rocks sound like? What noise to rocks make? They are quiet! When rocks shout, interestingly they are silent. Silent! Yet maybe their silence is their judgement against us. Could it be that silence, even the silence of the stones and rocks shouting, is a witness against the injustice practiced by their human counterparts in God's creation. Yes, the silence of the rocks, can testify to our injustice and our inhumanity.

This summer I was struck twice within 24 hours by the sound of silence. I heard the silence. I heard the rocks. Silence! One Tuesday evening this summer, while in Jacksonville, FL, attending the Annual Conference of the International Council of Community Church, I had a phone conversation with my daughter, Sara, who was living in The Bronx, NY. She was spending a year living in the Morrisania neighborhood of The Bronx serving in the Episcopal Youth Service Corp, living in religious community with other Corp members in an old church rectory. She lived in an immigrant neighborhood, mostly people of Puerto Rican, Dominican, Jamaican, Haitian and Antiguan ancestry. Most weekends in the warm months the neighborhood is alive on Saturday nights - grills on sidewalks, music from car speakers, baseball games in the street or parks. It's a weekly celebration of life! Almost like an American tail gate party without the football game. The celebrations start in the late afternoon, maybe 3:00 or 4:00 P.M., and last into the night, maybe 2:00 or 3:00 A.M. Since the old rectory where she lives has no air conditioning, the music lingering into her bedroom window until 3:00 A.M. does little for sleep.

But the weekend before our phone conversation was a time when the Trump administration had threatened large-scale immigration raids in major cities across the country. That Saturday evening as Sara was returning home from spending the day passing out English/Spanish immigrant help sheets, telling people what to do and who to call if ICE came to their door or arrested a loved one, she passed a park usually filled with people on a late Saturday afternoon. It was about empty. A small baseball game was being played with far less people than usual, but that was all. Much quieter than usual. As she walked the sidewalks down the last few blocks to her house the sidewalks were empty. No grills. No sidewalk food. No cars blasting music. No baseball games in the street. Silence! That Saturday night no music floated into her bedroom window until 3:00 A.M. Silence! It was the silence of fear. It was the silence of injustice. I'm sure amid the silence the stones where shouting judgement against our inhumanity. Silence! During that phone call on the following Tuesday I was shocked, saddened, troubled by what I heard her describe. I could not get her story out of my mind.

Turn the clock ahead 16 hours, just 16 hours. I heard it! I heard the silence all the way in Jacksonville, FL. That next day the International Council of Community Churches (ICCC) held a prayer gathering at The Jacksonville Landing, a former shopping and restaurant venue in downtown Jacksonville. Just eleven months earlier a mass shooting took place at The Landing at a pizza restaurant, during a video football gaming competition, at which two people were killed and ten wounded. Of course, that tragedy made national news as one of the many mass shootings of 2018. The day we gathered, we gathered at noon, the time when The Jacksonville Landing would have usually been at its busiest. The Landing sits on the riverfront of the St. John's

River, on a beautiful Riverwalk. It had stores for shopping. It had restaurants for lunch as businesspeople from downtown Jacksonville would have flooded The Landing each day at Noon. It was a bustling, vibrant venue for downtown Jacksonville. A place of fun and life, until August 26, 2018. After the shootings, the crowds left, and the shops and restaurants began to close. A couple weeks before I was there the last restaurant closed. The week before my visit the city of Jacksonville purchased the property and now plans its demolition. I was there with my siblings in the ICCC at noon that day to pray– at noon! Noon, the time of past hurriedness and vitality. Instead – Silence. Silence! Literally in the middle of an outdoor mall in the downtown of a big city – Silence. Again, it was the silence of fear. It was the silence of injustice. I'm sure amid the silence the stones where shouting from the St. John's riverbanks judgement against our inhumanity. Silence!

After the time of prayer, I wandered around The Landing. While standing down by the river I met a security guard named Tony. After some other conversation and answering his question on why a pastor from Iowa was wandering in downtown Jacksonville, I asked about the shooting. Tony was working on that day and saw the shooter. Tony walked me up to the restaurant, Chicago Pizza, where the mass shooting occurred. Tony told me the gunman had lost a significant amount of money in the video football competition that day and was angry at the last man who beat him. He left the restaurant to return to his hotel to get a knife and a gun. Returning to the restaurant first with the knife he was met with laugher. He quickly left. Minutes later he returned with a gun and began shooting. Twelve people were shot, two fatally. As the gunman left the restaurant and was on the sidewalk outside, Tony saw him still with a gun in hand. Tony was about 50 to 60 feet away across the street. As a security guard Tony had bullets and a gun, but only police are permitted to carry loaded guns, so Tony's gun was unloaded. The gunman looked at Tony and could have shot at him, but at that moment a SWAT team appeared running down the street and the gunman quickly turned to see those SWAT members approaching. At that point the gunman took his gun and shot himself. As Tony describes this, I quickly ask, "Where did he shoot himself?" Tony's answer, "About right here. Right about where we are standing now." Something came over me. Maybe it was the silence. I thanked Tony. I wished him well. I really couldn't bear to stand there anymore. I have found myself standing on holy ground many times, but this was not one of those moments. I was beyond words. I was silent as I walked away.

Jesus was never fond of silence nor inaction. Those Christians who seem to think that Jesus was some quiet, humble religious mystic who liked to pray by himself and was out to preserve a pious, Jewish religious tradition, might want to go back and read the Bible again. Within just five verses of Jesus' comment of the stones crying out to testify to the presence of God's reign, we find Jesus in the Jerusalem Temple driving people out. He wasn't silent. He saw how the money changers were cheating the people as they exchanged Roman coin for Temple coin. Jesus did not tolerate injustice. Jesus didn't walk off to the corner of the Temple to pray for an end to the unjust practices. He stood for justice and drove people of the Temple. Yes, Jesus, the one we call Child of the Living God, literally threw people out of God's house! Yes, he did!

Jesus showed us by word and action how to live into God's reign of love and justice. Jesus was never shy, never silent:

Jesus called King Herod a fox.
Jesus told Roman governor Pilate to his face that God's reign was not of this world.
Jesus touched the outcast leper.
Jesus told stories where the rich burned in Hades and the poor enjoyed paradise.
Jesus taught to love and pray for our enemies.
Jesus ignored unjust religious traditions and plucked grain to feed people on the Sabbath.
Jesus condemned the rich, the filled, and the laughing to instead bless the poor, the hungry and the mourning.

150

> Jesus constantly reinterpreted the Jewish Law by saying, "You have heard it said…but I say to you…"

Jesus was not silent. No stones needed to cry out when Jesus was around.

In the last two months I have not only visited the site of the Jacksonville mass shooting, but I have visited other "silent" places, some while doing ecumenical work for the ICCC in our witness to unity and reconciliation. In just the last two months I have stood at the site of the assassination of the Rev. Dr. Martin Luther King in Memphis. I have walked the Edmund Pettus Bridge and stood at the site of Bloody Sunday in Selma, Alabama. I have visited Ground Zero in New York and heard the voices reading names of loved ones and seeing the wall of pictures of those lost to evil on 9/11. I have walked the hanging columns and saw the DNA-dirt filled jars of the "Lynching Memorial", or properly named the National Memorial for Peace and Justice in Montgomery, Alabama. I walked the Great Hall of Ellis Island where thousands of immigrants once passed, while on the same day news reports continued to tell us how today's immigrants are being locked in cages like animals at the US southern border. I have heard the silence! The stones have shouted loud their witness to our inhumanity. The silence witnesses to our injustice was hard to "hear". At times the silence was deafening!

The Church has many struggles in today's world. In recent months the Church has worked tirelessly on behalf of migrants, providing food, shelter, sanctuary, legal counsel, and bandaging what the US government is wounding. The task right now is overwhelming as our Christian siblings are being arrested and charged for giving food, drink and basic medical care to migrants, and Christian clergy are under surveillance by the government for their ministry among migrants. The church is acting, we are not silent.

But the Gospel of Jesus the Christ calls us to be the constant presence and voice of Jesus in all things:

151

+ As drums of war beat, the Church must speak and act.

+ As creation is attacked, the Church must speak and act.

+ As the plague of guns kills American society, the Church must speak and act.

+ As the mentally ill have care taken from them, the Church must speak and act.

+ As racism is encouraged, the Church must speak and act.

+ As the rich get richer and the poor and hungry are forgotten, the Church must speak and act.

+ As LGBTQ+ persons are attacked and basic human rights denied them, the Church must speak and act.

+ As migrants are villainized, and treated as sub-human, the Church must speak and act.

+ As basic health care and its surrounding technologies are not available to every person, the Church must speak and act.

There can be no silence on these and many other parts of our human life.

Plus, the Church must examine itself, its own silence about itself and its history:

+There can be no more silence on the Church's love of earthly power and wealth.

+There can be no more silence on the Church's sexual abuse of its members.

+There can be no more silence on the Church's treatment of women as second-class members of creation.

+ There can be no more silence on the Church's treatment of LGBTQ+ persons as persons not equally created in God's image.

+ There can be no more silence on the Church's treatment of people of various races and ethnic groups using the excuse of theological doctrine of white European patriarchy and privilege.

The opposite of silence is sound and celebration. Jesus came that we may have life in all its abundance and fulness (John 10:10). The meaning of the Gospel of Jesus the Christ is getting us out of the silence of our brokenness and into the sound of the fulness of God's restored life. God's salvation is that healing, that reconciliation, that process of restoration, that takes us from silence to celebration, from brokenness to wholeness.

By our work of proclaiming and living the Gospel, the sounds of silence will grow into the rowdy shouts of God's justice and a chorus of love and shalom for all God's creation!

2021 SERMONS & REFLECTIONS

Rev. Regina Maria Cross, MS
Sparrow Hawk Village
Tahlequah, Oklahoma

GIVING THANKS

In the Glory of God
I Give Thanks
In the Sadness of Life
I Give Thanks
In the Joy of Moments
I Give Thanks
In the Magic of Everyday Life
I Give Thanks
For no apparent reason
I Give Thanks
Because there is Always Reason
To Give Thanks

Passing the Mantle
2 KINGS 2: 1–12; MARK 9: 2–9

Joe Sellepeck

I have always loved our reading today from 2 Kings. The story is about an older prophet passing on his authority and position to a younger one. Elijah passing his ministry to Elisha.

It's almost indicative in their names, right? Elijah sounds so much like Elisha that we often confuse the two. We hear a story and we think, wasn't that Elijah? No it was Elisha... And we see the two almost through the same lens. And so we should, because this story, while it is about passing a ministry of prophecy from one person to another, it is more about God's faithfulness to God's people in raising up ordained prophets who will lead their people into faithful service. God is the focus of this story and the orchestration behind it. God, after all, ordains prophets. In this story the prophets Elijah and Elisha journey together through the history of the Israelite people. They see Jericho and Gilgal. They journey to Bethel. They come to the Jordan River and the river parts when Elijah strikes it with his mantle. Here in these few sentences, the writer of the story is asking the reader to remember all of the amazing stories of faith that took place.

Jericho is the place of Israel's greatest victory. The people walk around the city and the walls come tumbling down. Gilgal was the first permanent camp that Israel had in the promised land. It was the first place that the Hebrew people celebrated the Passover when they crossed the Jordan river. It is Bethel where Jacob sees the angel of God ascending and descending the ladder between earth and heaven. It this place Bethel where Jacob and his predecessor Abraham talked with God. Elijah and Elisha walk through this history on their journey before Elijah is taken up in the fiery chariot and Elisha picks up the mantle. This is a mantle of faith. It is a mantle of leadership. It is a mantle of love and promise between God and God's people. God will not leave them without a leader. Elisha would take up the mantle and lead when Elijah has left the scene and gone up to be with God.

In many ways this is also what happens on the Mountainside during the Transfiguration. Up until this week, I had never really asked the question, how did Peter know that it was Elijah and Moses that appear with Jesus on the Holy Mountain? I mean, it isn't that Peter had been introduced to them. They didn't have cameras that would have taken pictures of them. There were no artistic depictions at the time. We have some today that tell us what people thought they looked like, but how did Peter know then? But the text says that Peter sees two flaming, glowing people being transfigured with Jesus and intuitively knows that they are Elijah and Moses.

And maybe that is the point. Viewed through the eyes of faith and history, it all comes together at this moment for Peter. Elijah and Moses are passing on the mantle to Jesus, and those who follow the history, those who know the story, those who are enraptured by the faith know who these people are. So it shouldn't surprise us that God's voice comes into the story and tells us to listen to Jesus: "Here is my beloved son, listen to him!"

Peter knows because he has been listening to these stories all of his life. He knows because it resonates from deep within him. He knows because this is the trajectory of all that he has been waiting for, watching for, working for, from his Bar Mitzvah until his calling to follow Jesus. Everything about Peter's life led him to this moment. And in this moment, concentrated in Jesus, all of the stories of his life and faith made sense.

I too have had these experiences. I can name them in my head and they have become the stories of my faith. Today I want to tell you one of them. In my mind thirty years later, I see a man named Lenny Brickhandler who I met in Chicago. He was a near homeless senior citizen who had lived for many years in an SRO (Single Room

Occupancy). His paltry social security checks paid for that room and little else. Like many Seniors on the North Side of Chicago, Lenny depended upon the senior citizen's program at LaSalle Street Church for food and fellowship. When I met him Lenny had just suffered a major stroke and was in a long term care facility. This left half of his body paralyzed and the stroke really did a number on his emotions. He couldn't get through a conversation without bursting intermittently into fits of tears and laughter. I was an intern at LaSalle Street Church and had the responsibility of pastoring many of those like Lenny who were shut in and not able to get to church. Lenny was the first visit I ever did at a Nursing home and he made an indelible impression on my life. While visiting with him I peeled away the layers of his life. While many saw him as just a homeless man who was near death, I saw him as a veteran of WW2. He had served in the European Theater and had helped liberate people from concentration camps. In his earlier life, he had been a laborer, working construction jobs that helped build the city of Chicago. He loved chocolate and sweets. He was a good friend to several people in the Senior Center. Scratch the surface, look beneath into the interior of his life. Lenny was a child of God. A person of great worth. Someone who should be listened to.

When this really came home to me was at Christmastime. Shelly had just made a plate of her grandfather's peanut butter fudge. It probably isn't the best fudge you will ever eat, but Grandpa Mark didn't cook very often. Encie, his wife, did most of that. But every year Grandpa Beecher would brush off the apron and make peanut butter fudge and give it as a present to family members at Christmas. Shelly's mother had asked him to pass on the recipe to her and she had given these family recipes to Shelly as a wedding gift. Shelly had made a large batch for Christmas presents and she gave me a smallish plate to take to Lenny. When I entered Lenny's room at the nursing home, the smell of ammonia and disinfectant was incredibly strong. The nurse told me that one of Lenny's roommates had just wet the bed and they had to clean it up. So I waited in the hallway until everything inside was copacetic.

When I entered the room, I placed the peanut butter fudge on the nightstand next to Lenny's bed. This was Lenny's non-paralyzed side, the place where he placed all of his mementos and the TV remote that made his life better. I reached over and shook his hand then we started to talk. He told me the stories of his life, probably for the seventh or eighth time since I had met him. Through fits of tears and laughter, he relayed all of the stories that he rehearsed in his head that told who he was, what he had done, and what he hoped for. I listened and then told him the story of the peanut butter fudge and how the recipe was passed on from Shelly's grandfather. He started to cry. Tears streamed down his face. I couldn't find any Kleenex to give him to wipe his face, so I went out to the nurse's station to ask for some. They gave me a box and I walked back into the room. By the time I returned, all six pieces of peanut butter fudge on that plate were gone. And Lenny had a smug, contented look about him. I handed him a Kleenex and together we wiped the tears and the crumbs from his face. And suddenly, at that moment, I realized what we had just done. It was a holy moment. A faith moment. A moment of transcendence and deep mystery. A transfiguration had just happened.

Peanut butter fudge, our personal stories of faith, and the grace of God's presence converged in that ammonia scented nursing home. The veil was ripped away between Lenny and me and I realized that Christ was present in the breaking of the bread. We had just experienced all of the stories of faith, of death and life, and the mystery of Divine presence. This was an epiphany, a divine moment where the veil between this life and the next was wafer thin and life became deeper and more holy than I could even articulate. Now tears were streaming down my face, and I needed the Kleenex. While I had passed the mantle of peanut butter fudge, Lenny had given me the gift of his story, his presence, and his faith. We had experienced communion together. And while I didn't hear it physically, I truly did in spirit. In that moment God said, "This is my beloved Son, Lenny Brickhandler, listen to him."

In many ways this is what we do for each other in church. We listen to our stories. We sit with each other and allow God's holiness, our personal stories, and the stories of our faith to converge. They become so close together that we only have one word in the English language that even approximates the beauty and mystery that transpires between us. That word is love. Love breaks through the barriers and shows us the depths of what we need to know about our past, what we yearn for in our present, and what we hope for in our future. It is love which called out to Peter when Jesus was transfigured and made him know that it was Elijah and Moses. It was love that was passed on from Elijah to Elisha when the mantle of his ministry was passed. Love passed down through the generations as Grandfather gave the peanut butter fudge recipe to daughter-in-law and finally to granddaughter. It was love that broke the veil between a near homeless man named Lenny Brickhandler and me. It was love. It is love. It always will be love.

That would be the last time that I ever saw Lenny Brickhandler alive. When I went back after Christmas, they informed me that Lenny had died. The social worker did not have me listed as a person to call, nor did they know of his history with the LaSalle Street Church Senior Center. So we were not informed. At the next opportunity, I told Lenny's story to the seniors who were gathered at breakfast one Sunday morning at LaSalle Street Church. I told them how a man named Lenny Brickhandler had revealed God's Holiness and presence to me. I told them of that great word that brings it all together in our lives: Love. And I told them that this is the gift that we give to each other, that makes the veil between us a little thinner, and that sums up what our past is, what we most want presently, and what all of our hopes and dreams for the future are.

And friends this same love is the mantle we pass to each other today. It is our gift that we present to each other on this Transfiguration Sunday. This love is expressed in tenderness and gifts of bread and wine that we give to each other.

160

And so I invite you to the deep mystery of our faith. I invite you to experience the thinning veil between God and us and us from each other. I invite you to see each other as of Holy and supreme worth. I invite you to a Transfiguration of Divine Love where we see each other for who we truly are.

Even today, friends, Peanut Butter Fudge is being transformed into a gift of mystery and grace. Life will never be the same after this moment we have with each other. Together we can hear and see each other as we truly are and be marked by tenderness and God's presence. And together we can hope for a time when all of God's children will be treated with dignity and respect. We can pass that mantle of love to each other that welcomes and includes and listens to each other's stories.

All I know is that for me, Peanut Butter Fudge will never be the same.

Faithful to Reconciliation
MATTHEW 5:23-26

Abraham Wright

> Gert told Net that if she needed her, call her.
> The last thing Gert said as Net walked out the door was,
> "Net, did you hear what I said?"
> Very lowly, Net replied, "Yes."
> But six months passed;
> Net has been in several desperate situations,
> but she has **not** called Gert.

How many of you know of situations like this? How many of you have among your immediate families, your church family, and your friends those who make promises to you but you don't call them in times of trouble because you know they won't respond favorably, or they will help you like the Christians characterized in 1 Corinthians 13 who speak with the tongues of men and of angels, who have the gift of prophecy and enough knowledge to remove mountains, and give their bodies to be burned but they post their helping you out on the Internet faster than a heavy rock sinks to the bottom of a lake? And yet we wonder why there is a breach between us and them: Why can't we just get along? Why can't we forgive and forget; then, go back and remember for the rest of our lives things that happened before Methuselah was born?

Have we not heard the gospel news of the clear call of reconciliation in the body of Christ, beginning with Jesus as a ransom for our sins and moving forward to our becoming agents/ambassadors of reconciliation for Jesus Christ? So if you have ears, lend them to me for the next 20 minutes. If you have not, be curious and listen anyway; you might avoid an egregious sin by doing so.

The scripture reference is 2 Corinthians 5:17-20a with emphasis on 19b and 20a: "And he has committed to us the message of reconciliation. We are therefore Christ's ambassadors, as though God were making his appeal through us." Christ grants us the ministry of reconciliation between God and human, among humans, and with all creation. That includes social justice, inequity, and all the ism's. The old is done away with; the new is in with no distinction between Jews and Gentiles, no separation between the residents of Potomac, Maryland and Southeast Washington, DC or Watts (Los Angeles), California and Irvine, California, between 125th Street in Harlem and the Hamptons, Long Island, New York. That gap is closed. Our whole way of thinking and feeling and acting are new. So if you danced previously left to right, you now go up and down unless you make it clear that the left-to-right movements are the gen-u-(w)ine Holy Spirit.

When God reconciled us through the death and resurrection of Jesus Christ, He gave Paul and Paul's fellow evangelists the task to announce the plan with expectation of a response from us to "be reconciled to God" (2 Cor. 5:20). This essentially means getting rid of all kinds of sin and living a life worthy of the redemptive state to which Christ called us, so that others would want to be a part of us and not be tagged with names that degrade and isolate them; for both of us are heirs of the Kingdom, just like Prince Charles and Meghan Markel.

Dr. Benda Salter believes that in the process of reconciliation, we want people not just to sit down together but "relate to each other, to identify with each other"; we want to care about each other. We want to avoid the "fix-it" solution. We come to learn ways of getting to the root of the problem so we can tell it to go to the bottomless pit. We want to walk beside them because we don't have all the answers; for in some ways our predicament is just like theirs; so we validate them by regarding them as assets instead of liabilities. When we both put on some humility and begin to risk the chance of trusting each other; then, just maybe then, God will recognize our genuineness, and grant us healing grace. This reaching out to the other side is to be done graciously and intentionally because it ties in with the mission of God in that, as Salter observes, we are to "preach and teach radical discipleship with Christ and costly peacemaking as the norm of Christian faith." We must name the egregious wrong, confess it, and act on it. ICCC prides itself as a communion whose heart is reconciliation of the body of Christ. So we must be the body that we

163

profess to be worthy of our name. As Bruce Merton often says, "I see, See, See (ICCC)."

This includes things such as giving a worthy graduate student a pulpit to fulfill an assigment when all other churches reject him or her as an inexperienced preacher who probably preaches as well as an experienced one. It is ICCC answering the prayer of Maurice McCracken, American civil rights and peace activist Presbyterian minister whose Presbytery of Cincinnati defrocked him from the Community Church of Cincinnati in West End for his protest of the Vietnam War. Yes, twenty-five years later, the Presbyterian Church restored Maurice, admitting that his defrocking was an error; but can you imagine what might have happened to Maurice emotionally had ICCC not been an agent of reconciliation who reached out and joined hand with Maurice to make his life better? I don't want ICCC to be too proud, but you must admit that in order to participate in the act of reconciliation, you must first be reconciled yourself.

Michael Bird observes that reconciliation does not take so much humility on the part of the receiver but on the giver, the one who is touched with the Holy Spirit to initiate the act; and the ICCC family has been touched by several reconciling souls. For example, Dr. Marion C. Bascom, a distinguished clergy in Baltimore, fought fiercely for racial justice, and used Douglas Memorial Community Church as one of the major civil rights stations in Baltimore. Douglas also was often used for COCU/CUIC national and area meetings and for meetings of the National Council of Churches, USA. In a similar spirit of reconciliation during the 1970s, Rev. Dr. William Samuels, an avid drum major for social justice, worked with youth for Rainbow PUSH and the Rev. Jessie Jackson.

Reconciliation is the Rev. Dr. Jeffrey Newhall, the "pink" ICCC Executive Director who was the equity pastors' shepherd, regardless of their color, class, or culture. Reconciliation is ICCC reaching out to worthy clergy and making it possible for those who might have been displaced or defrocked to see clearly God as the God of a Second and a Third Chance. Yes, reconciliation is:

1. Forgiving and remembering only if remembering sheds light on the present, causing the relationship to bring us closer to Christ or to a resolution.

2. It's an ICCC military retired chaplain contacting a former supervisor who tried to wreck his career, and talk about old times and express his concern for the former supervisor's well being.

3. It's an ICCC ordained Florida clergy taking a backseat and becoming Secretary of the Council, which opened the door for a lay person to become President.

4. Reconciliation is an Executive Director having his salary reduced by almost three quarters in one fiscal year but worked as hard as he did before the reduction, for the sake of reconciliation.

5. Reconciliation is not puffing up the person who initiates the act but uplifting the individual who is being welcomed or reinstated into the family of believers.

6. Reconciliation is taking the Lord's Supper at a table where you genuinely repent of your sins and ask for forgiveness and are equally welcome with other children of God.

7. Reconciliation is staying awake each night for the 11:00 o'clock news to join a group of senior clergy on the streets of Baltimore to ensure that media, who tended to sensationalize acts of violence, did not exploit African American young males by inciting more violence.

So as the Old Testament prophets had a passion for social justice, as Jesus walked among and associated with the outcast, the dispossessed, the lame, the blind, Rahab, the woman with an issue of blood, the woman at the well, the tax collector, and the thief on the cross who is saved at Jesus' crucifixion; and as He walks with us and reconciles so many broken relationships today, let us rekindle our passion, as if God were speaking to us at this very moment, and continue the work of reconciliation that there might be no division among us.

Where ALL Are Welcome:
A Communion Sermon
ISAIAH 25:6-9

Rev. Robert Fread
Hudson, Iowa
ICCC Clergy Special Standing
Pastor, Union Congregational United Church of Christ, Reinbeck, IA

The Table is set. The Feast is spread. ALL are welcome! Come!
We have just sung the words of Marty Haugen, a contemporary,
liturgical hymn writer, from his hymn, "*All Are Welcome*":

> Let us build a house where love is found
> In water, wine and wheat:
> A banquet hall on holy ground,
> Where peace and justice meet.
> Here the love of God, through Jesus,
> Is revealed in time and space.
> As we share in Christ the feast that frees us:
> All are welcome, all are welcome, All are welcome in this place.
> © 1994 GIA Publications Inc.

During the summer of 2019 on my way to be part of the International
Council of Community Churches' delegation to the Plenary of
Churches Uniting in Christ in Montgomery, Alabama, I decided to
drive to Montgomery via Selma, and re-trace the route of the historic
Selma to Montgomery Marches of 1965. I began at the Brown Chapel
African Methodist Episcopal Church in Selma, where all three
marches began. I then dove the few blocks to the Edmund Pettus
Bridge, there parking my car, to make the sacred pilgrimage of
walking over the bridge. Walking that bridge is a holy experience.
Once over the bridge I walked back to retrieve my car and continue
the journey. I then drove over the bridge, stopping at a small park
tucked under the south side of the bridge containing monuments
related to the march, including to the original march leaders, John

Lewis and Rev. Hosea Williams. After some time reflecting in the park, as I returned to my car, I encountered a man named Columbus. Columbus sold souvenirs out of a nearby building and described himself as caretaker of the park. As Columbus and I chatted, he told me about his Uncle Willie Thornton (his father's brother). Uncle Willie was a combat veteran from the Korean War. Upon returning home from the war, Uncle Willie worked on his farm and was involved in the Civil Rights Movement. On March 7, 1965, Uncle Willie was one of the 600 marchers who left the Brown Chapel AME Church, walked through the streets of downtown Selma, and walked over the Pettus Bridge on that infamous Bloody Sunday. At the peak of the bridge, they could see the Alabama State Troopers waiting for them. They continued to walk about a half mile down from the bridge until stopped by the state troopers. The marchers stopped to pray as authorities ordered John Lewis and Rev. Williams to disband the march. Uncle Willie told Columbus that Lewis and Williams were told they had two minutes to disband. But then about 30 seconds later, before the prayers were ended, troopers began beating the marchers. John Lewis' skull was fractured. Uncle Willie was struck by a trooper in the eye. Uncle Willie never had vision in that eye again. After Bloody Sunday, Uncle Willie returned to his farm, blind in one eye, to raise food, as Columbus put it, "for everyone who needed it, black or white". Every day Columbus stands at the base of that holy bridge to tell visitors about what happened there and to keep the memory of his Uncle Willie alive. Uncle Willie could be sent to a land far away to "fight for his country", but it was a country who did not want him here. His own country inflicted permanent physical damage on him that some "foreign enemy" did not. Uncle Willie was not welcome in his own country. He stood for civil rights, but he was not welcome at the lunch counter, the bathroom, or the drinking fountain. He stood bloodied and blinded for voting rights, but he was not welcome in a voting booth! SOME PEOPLE ARE JUST NOT WELCOME!

Let us not forget that the Church of Jesus Christ has a long history of not welcoming "certain" people. Yes, not welcome in the church. Not welcome at the font. Not welcome at the Lord's Table. Not welcome because of race, ethnic origin, economic status, sexual orientation, gender, gender identity, theology, etc.... Tragically and sinfully the church has mentally and spiritually bloodied and blinded many people in letting them know that the church was NOT a place of welcome for them. The sin of centuries of injustice: sexism, racism, classism, homophobia, etc... has spiritually beaten many people to drive them away from the church. In the name of Jesus, the Christ- ALL MUST BE WELCOME!

The Gospel of Jesus is clear that all persons are equally made and loved by God. This was proclaimed by the church from the beginning. In Acts, Peter in his sermon to the first Gentile Christians is clear, "I truly understand that God shows no partiality." (Acts 10:34b) and Paul in his sermon in Athens says, "From one ancestor (God) made all nations to inhabit the whole earth." (Acts 17:26a)

Just six weeks after walking the Edmund Pettus Bridge in Selma, I found myself in a quite different location, but a holy spot none the less. I was representing the ICCC as an ecumenical guest at the General Assembly of the Christian Church (Disciples of Christ) in Des Moines, Iowa. Worship for the assembly was being held in the Wells Fargo Sports Arena. As I entered the 15,000-seat arena for worship, before me was a wonderful sight. A large round table filled with wheat and grapes, bread, chalices, and candles literally in the center of the arena. I have watched sporting events in that arena before and that beautiful table was standing at what would normally be the center of the basketball court or the red line at a hockey game. Yet on this night in the center of that sports arena was a bountiful, overflowing table – calling to ALL, welcoming ALL, ready to give nourishment to ALL who would come. Truly a holy sight! I knew I was welcome.

Yet in a moment while looking at that welcoming, holy table, I flashed back to many times I was not welcome at the Lord's Table in some denominations, and to those in our society who still don't feel welcome in the church. But on that night, that table invited everyone

ALL genders and gender identities, ALL races, ethnic and national backgrounds, ALL sexual orientations, ALL economic situations – it called to ALL! ALL are welcome!

The image of feast and table have always been a key symbol within the Judeo-Christian tradition. The feast, or the table filled, is a historic image of the fulness and invitation to God's salvation - God's healing and reconciliation. In the Bible where there is a table, there is often a feast where God is encountered, and people are filled and made whole.

As we are gathered at the Lord's Table this morning, gathered to celebrate this holy and life-giving Sacrament, know that God is present. We hear in Isaiah this morning:

> "On this mountain the LORD of hosts will *make for all peoples* a feast of rich food, a feast of well-aged wines, of rich food filled with marrow, of well-aged wines strained clear…It will be said on that day, Lo, this is our God; we have waited for him, so that he might save us. This is the LORD for whom we have waited; let us be glad and rejoice in his salvation."
> (Isaiah 25:6,9)

Did you hear that! God will make a feast for all people. For ALL people! ALL are welcome!

This Table, standing before us this morning in this century old sanctuary, is holding the feast of love, salvation, and life. God has set this feast. God has invited us. Here at this table, you are welcome to come. Here at this Table, you are welcome to be nourished. Here at this Table, you are welcome to find a Love that made you and holds you.

Come to this table! ALL are welcome!

Thus Far the LORD Has Helped Us.

1 SAMUEL 7:3-12, NRSV

Ron Sinclair

Then Samuel said to all the house of Israel, "If you are returning to the Lord with all your heart, then put away the foreign gods and the Astartes from among you. Direct your heart to the Lord, and serve him only, and he will deliver you out of the hand of the Philistines." So Israel put away the Baals and the Astartes, and they served the Lord only. Then Samuel said, "Gather all Israel at Mizpah, and I will pray to the Lord for you." So they gathered at Mizpah, and drew water and poured it out before the Lord. They fasted that day, and said, "We have sinned against the Lord." And Samuel judged the people of Israel at Mizpah.

The raiders of the lost Ark had returned it to the defeated Israelites.

Israelite forces had been defeated near a place called Ebenezer. Then they brought the Ark of the Covenant to their camp, tried to use it like a magical amulet with the help of two dull witted priests, the sons of an ineffective high priest, Eli. They tried to harness the Ark's power. You already know how this turned out don't you? (You've seen the movie!) The Israelites lost the battle, the high priest's sons lost their lives, and the Ark of the Covenant was captured.

Having captured it, the Philistines tried to use it, to manipulate its power. They suffered or died trying to do that. They sent the Ark back home to the Israelites with expensive gifts. Twenty years passed while an entire generation longed for God. Then the prophet Samuel called the people together for repentance and they did repent with fasting and confession of sin. This might be a good place to end the story, but it gets so much better!

When the Philistines heard that the people of Israel had gathered at Mizpah, the lords of the Philistines went up against Israel. And when the people of Israel heard of it they were afraid of the Philistines. The people of Israel said to Samuel, "Do not cease to cry out to the Lord our God for us, and pray that he may save us from the hand of the Philistines." So Samuel took a suckling lamb and offered it as a whole burnt offering to the Lord; Samuel cried out to the Lord for Israel, and the Lord answered him. As Samuel was offering up the burnt offering, the Philistines drew near to attack Israel; but the Lord thundered with a mighty voice that day against the Philistines and threw them into confusion; and they were routed before Israel. And the men of Israel went out of Mizpah and pursued the Philistines, and struck them down as far as beyond Beth-car. Then Samuel took a stone and set it up between Mizpah and Jeshanah, and named it Ebenezer; for he said, "Thus far the Lord has helped us."

The raiders of the Ark were routed. The Israelites remembered because of a stone.

The God of heaven's voice thundered and it was enough, more than enough. Samuel set up a stone and named it, Ebenezer. Ebenezer means, stone of help. The Israelites would see that stone and remember God's help for generations.

"Thus far the Lord has helped us."

The Lord helps those who renounce false gods. May we never worship worldly powers whether military, industrial, political, financial, or spiritual nor even presidents, political parties, flags, banners, and lawn signs with our favorite person's names, T-shirts with hateful cryptic messages, websites with secret conspiracy theories, or 24 hour news channels whether their news is real or fake.

"*Thus far* the Lord has helped us."

Let us not tempt the Lord our God!
In the past, God has blessed a nation dedicated to a peaceful transfer of power. Will God still bless us? I hope so. What strengthens my hope? Two fellows named Jon and Raphael.

Jon's mom immigrated from Australia. His dad is of Russian and Lithuanian Jewish descent. He grew up amongst older people who were Holocaust survivors; it made an impression. While in high school he interned with a senator named John Lewis who had also known persecution. Later he served as a National Security staffer and aide to a US Congressional Representative. He also earned a masters degree in economics. Jon went on to marry his high school sweetheart and to lose a massively expensive election in 2017. In 2021 he became the first Jewish U.S. senator ever elected from Georgia.

Raphael is the eleventh of twelve children born to two bi-vocational Pentecostal pastors, so why didn't they name him Joseph? He has said that his mother used to pick cotton, but a few days back she picked him at the polls. He'll be the first African American US Senator Georgia ever elected. He's the pastor of Ebenezer Baptist Church in Atlanta. Ebenezer.

"Thus far the Lord has helped us."

The Rev. Dr. Raphael Warnock and Jon Ossoff will soon serve together in a country that struggles, sometimes successfully, to be a "government of the people, by the people, for the people"; all the people.

Raphael and Jon call to mind a two other people, Martin and Abraham. In January of 1963, Rabbi Abraham Joshua Heschel gave the speech "Religion and Race" at a conference that assembled in Chicago. There he met Dr. Martin Luther King, Jr. and the two became friends. 1963? Fifty-eight years ago. In 1965 Rabbi Heschel marched with Dr. King in Selma, Alabama. That was march took place over fifty-five years ago.

Could Martin and Abraham have imagined in their time what would happen in Georgia in 2021 or in Washington D.C. on Epiphany this past January 6? We all know Martin had a dream. King and Rabbi Heschel knew that racism was, to use Abraham's words, "a treacherous denial of the existence of God". They both knew the amazing heights we could aspire to and attain. They also knew the depths of our inhumanity and depravity. They knew their Bibles. Martin Luther King, Jr. was one of the pastors of Ebenezer Baptist Church the day he was assassinated. Ebenezer.

"Thus far the Lord has *helped us*."

God does help us, but God's people may suffer all manner of deprivation and persecution, even death.

The biblical vision of shalom: flourishing abundance, justice, mercy, and peace takes time, many generations. It's worth the wait. It's worth the work; both on our knees in prayer and on our feet to move forward.

"Thus far the Lord has helped us."

Living and True God, help our nation again as you have helped it thus far. Amen.

Still Standing There?
ACTS 1: 1 – 11
A Sermon for Ascension Sunday

Rev. Donald H. Ashmall
ICCC Council Minister Emeritus

If the life of Jesus, and the scripture we just read, were all a three-act play, we'd be at the end of the third act, just before the curtain went down. The play opened with a high-tension pregnancy announcement and an unusual birth, followed by a high-speed run to a foreign nation as a temporary refugee. And the play continued through visits to a temple; travels across hills and mountains; more than one boat trip; a betrayal; a violent death; and a discovery that love conquers even the worst that we can imagine, in a resurrection that broadcasts hope across the ages.

And so the final curtain comes down, and the disciples – and we – are transfixed and our mouths are hanging open, and we haven't moved. And then the theater ushers come by and ask us: why are you still standing there? Hold that thought while I do some reminiscing.

Back in the day a half century ago, when my first child was born, daddies were not allowed into the hospital delivery room. Period. No exceptions. Now, during my days in seminary, along with the rest of my peers I had spent a semester in hands-on training, learning counseling as a student chaplain in a hospital. And the ward I was assigned to was Boston City Hospital's 72 bed maternity ward. What do you mean I can't be in the delivery room? No. Those were the rules. And there was another rule for daddies. At least during the baby's first day we weren't allowed to hold our babies. Instead, a nurse stood behind glass, holding my baby up so I could see him. My naked first born, a boy. And I looked at him. And of course, I counted: ten fingers, ten toes. Wow. The miracle of a new life. But after a while the nurse kind of moved around restlessly. Okay daddy, you've seen

175

the baby. Now, you need to get your act together and move along, and do whatever you need to do, because now, you are a parent.

Pregnancy is a drama for mom-to-be and dad-to-be, and all the surrounding family and friends. But when that drama is over and the baby is born, and you've counted all the fingers and toes: don't you have something to do? Why are you still standing there?

Enough about me. What about the disciples and the scripture of the morning?

The disciples lived in what they thought was a layer cake universe. The waters above the firmament and the waters below the firmament, and in between a third layer that was everything else: the earth and the seas and the sky and even the heavens. So when Jesus was taken from them after promising the Holy Spirit, they saw what they expected to see – Jesus being lifted up, into the heavens.

As for us: we know that "up" is a relative term. We live in a cosmos of galaxies and black holes and indescribable distances where there is no measurable gravity and so there is no up or down. We live in a universe that demands a God greater than all those light years and more than any quantum physics can measure – which makes the idea of a God who is more, caring for the least of us who are less, absolutely overwhelming to the point that we are awestruck. When we attempt to see the scriptural account in the light of a God so great, it's little wonder that we are stuck, just standing there with our mouths hanging open. Which makes the message of every messenger of God (every angel) all the more important. Why are you just standing there? You have a message to proclaim and a presence to share. Don't just stand there. Do something, for God's sake!

Not long after Christianity started to spread across the then known world, a few pious believers decided that they would imitate Jesus' forty days in the wilderness – go off to some deserted place and pray and meditate and be still. Except some of them never came back. They stayed out in the wilderness and kept on meditating and praying

176

and seeking blessed visions. Other devout Christians would bring them food and encourage those hermits, some of whom attracted other hermits to live out there too, and together they became monastic communities that just kept to themselves and spent their entire lives praying and meditating.

Now far be it from me to criticize somebody else's piety, but I want to reach back through the centuries and shake them and say: "Read your scriptures!" There is a time to be enthralled by the beauty that God has given us, wherever we live. There is a time to meditate on God's goodness and mercy. There is a time to give thanks for blessings large and small. But at some point, the angels' question has to be asked: "what are you doing, still standing there?" All that you have received was not for you to hoard for yourself. Every gift of God is given to be shared.

Back to my reminiscing. I was in sixth grade, at Public School #22 in Yonkers, New York. There were about thirty kids in that classroom, 15 boys and 15 girls. At some point during the year, we were led downstairs to the gymnasium and informed that instead of our customary physical education activities, we were going to spend the next four weeks learning how to square dance. We were to line up in two lines by gender, and the person we were next to, in the other line, would be our partner for the four week period. And it turned out that my partner for the dance was Judy Wiggins. I do not remember the name of any other student who was in my class that year, and for the life of me I cannot recall the name of the teacher. And I don't care. But I remember Judy. Judy was to become my template for the ideal girlfriend, in appearance and voice and grace. And I got to square dance with her as my partner for a month that I hoped would never end.

I meditated on those dance sessions. I had visions, at twelve years old, of Judy in a wedding gown and us growing old together. I was enthralled. I was in rapture. And I never said a word to her that hinted at relationship. I was too shy, too withdrawn. I don't think I ever looked her in the eye. Judy never learned how I felt. And the next year we went on to different junior high schools in that city, and I never saw her again.

If my present-day self could communicate back through the years with my twelve-year old self, I would be shouting at myself: "why are you still standing there? You idiot!" Of course, it's just a childhood infatuation. Of course, it's just puppy love. But really, it isn't any of those; it isn't anything, unless you do something, say something.

Enough with the reminiscing.

All too often my present day relationship with God is too much like my long-ago relationship with Judy. True, I cannot reach out to hold the hand of Jesus; but I can hold the hand of one who is grieving and feeling lost and alone. I cannot give a hug to the man of Nazareth, but I can reach out to the hungry and the hurting. I cannot look the Master in the eye; but I can look into the eyes of one who has been excluded and demonized, and I can share acceptance and hope.

The one thing I must not do, dare not do, cannot do if my relationship with God is real, is to just keep standing there. Yes, I can pray in worship. Yes, I can look at the beauty of God's creation and give thanks. Yes, to all of that. But sooner or later some angel of God is going to ask me: "why are you still standing there? Worship is not complete until it issues into action. So, why are you still standing there?

Dr. Charles A. Trentham
Homiletics Award

The Charles A. Trentham Homiletics Award is an annual award given for the best sermon reflecting the spirit and values of the community church movement submitted each year for publication in the *Inclusive Pulpit Journal*. It is conferred at the Annual Conference of the International Council of Community Churches.

The Charles A. Trentham Homiletics Award Winners

1996 - No Award Given

1997 - Rev. Virginia Leopold "The Never Ending Journey"

1998 - Rev. Martin Singley, III, "Living in an Open Circle"

1999 - Rev. Herbert Freitag "Children of the Same God"

2000 - Rev. David H. Blanchett "A Single Point of Difference"

2001 - Rev. Robert A Fread "One Baptism"

2002 - Rev. C. David Matthews "Tragedy and God"

2003 - Dr. C. George Fry "God is Good - Always"

2004 - Dr. Jeffrey R. Newhall "Receiving into Our Heart"

2005 - Rev. Paul Drake "Unity in Diversity"

2006 - Dr. Keith R. Haverkamp "How Big Is Your Table"

2007 - Dr. Robert M. Puckett "To Be a Man"

2008 - Dr. William F. Schnell "One Church"

2009 - Rev. Harry Foockle "Obama, the ICCC and Me"

2010 - Rev. Martin Singley, III, "Skeletons in the Closet"

2011 - Chaplain Fran Salone-Pelletier, "Devoted to Community"

2012 - Rev. Rhonda Abbott Blevins, "What are you Doing Here?"

2013 - Rev. Dr. R. Timothy Meadows, "True Worship"

2014 - Rev. Herbert Freitag, "Jesus Might Be the Answer --- But What Is the Question"

2015 - Rev. Dr. William Schnell, "We Believe. In You"

2016 - Rev. Joseph D. Sellepack, "Words Fail, Love Wins"

2017 - Ella B. Clay, "God's Table Is Inclusive Of All Peoples"

2018 - Rev. Karen Neely, "Embrace"

2019 - Rev. Dr. Rhonda Abbott Blevins "When Pigs Fly"

2020 - Rev. Robert Fread, "The Sound of Silence: When Even the Stones Cry Out"

2021 - Rev. Don Ashmall, "Still Standing There?"